STAND OUT 2

Evidence-Based Learning for Life, College, and Career

FOURTH EDITION

ROB JENKINS

STACI JOHNSON

Australia • Brazil • Canada • Mexico • Singapore • United Kingdom • United States

National Geographic Learning,
a Cengage Company

Stand Out 2: Evidence-based Learning for Life, College, and Career, Fourth Edition
Rob Jenkins, Staci Johnson

Publisher: Sherrise Roehr

Executive Editor: Sarah Kenney

Managing Development Editor: Claudi Mimó

Director of Global Marketing: Ian Martin

Heads of Regional Marketing:
  Charlotte Ellis (Europe, Middle East and Africa)
  Justin Kaley (Asia and Greater China)
  Irina Pereyra (Latin America)
  Joy MacFarland (US and Canada)

Senior Content Project Manager: Beth McNally

Content Project Manager: Beth Houston

Media Researcher: Stephanie Eenigenburg

Art Director: Brenda Carmichael

Operations Support: Hayley Chwazik-Gee, Katie Lee

Manufacturing Planner: Mary Beth Hennebury

Composition: MPS North America LLC

© 2024 Cengage Learning, Inc.

ALL RIGHTS RESERVED. No part of this work covered by the copyright herein may be reproduced or distributed in any form or by any means, except as permitted by U.S. copyright law, without the prior written permission of the copyright owner.

"National Geographic", "National Geographic Society" and the Yellow Border Design are registered trademarks of the National Geographic Society
® Marcas Registradas

> For permission to use material from this text or product, submit all requests online at **cengage.com/permissions**
> Further permissions questions can be emailed to **permissionrequest@cengage.com**

Student's Book
ISBN: 978-0-357-96427-9
Student's Book with the Spark platform
ISBN: 978-0-357-96426-2

National Geographic Learning
200 Pier 4 Boulevard
Boston, MA 02210
USA

Locate your local office at **international.cengage.com/region**

Visit National Geographic Learning online at **ELTNGL.com**
Visit our corporate website at **www.cengage.com**

Printed in China
Print Number: 01 Print Year: 2023

Acknowledgments

Mai Ackerman
Ventura College; Los Angeles Mission College, CA

Raul Adalpe
Tarrant County College, Paradise, TX

Mariam Aintablian
Los Angeles Valley College, Valley Glen, CA

Steven Amos
Norfolk Public Schools/Adult Education Services, VA

Ana Arieli
College of Southern Nevada, Las Vegas, NV

Rachel Baiyor
Literacy Outreach, Glenwood Springs, CO

Gregory Baranoff
Santa Barbara City College, Santa Barbara, CA

Valerie Bare
Chesterfield County Public Schools, VA

Dyani Bartlett
Edmonds College, Lynnwood, WA

Karin Bates
Intercambio Uniting Communities, Boulder, CO

Robin Bitters
Adult Learning Program, Jamaica Plain Community Center, Putney, VT

Emily Bryson
ELT Specialist, Author, Teacher, Teacher Educator, Graphic Facilitator, ESOL Lecturer

Janelle Cardenas
Tarrant County College, TX

Joyce Clement
Chesterfield County Public Schools, VA

Juan Corona
Antelope Valley Adult School, Palmdale, CA

Vasilika Culaku
Goodwill, King County, Seattle, WA

Melinda Dart
Chesterfield County Public Schools, VA

Lourdes Davenport
Tarrant County College, TX

Geisa Dennis
Orange County Public Schools, Orlando, FL

Katie Donoviel
English Skills Learning Center, UT

Reyye Esat Yalcin
Bilingual Education Institute, Houston, TX

Aimee Finley
Dallas College, Dallas, TX

Eleanor Forfang-Brockman
Tarrant County College, Fort Worth, TX

Martha Fredendall
Literacy Outreach, Glenwood Springs, CO

Maria Gutierrez
Miami Sunset Adult Education Center, Miami, FL

Anne Henderson
Goodwill, King County, Seattle, WA

Tracey Higgins
Edmonds College, Lynnwood, WA

Daniel Hopkins
Tarrant County College, TX

Fayne Johnson
Atlantic Technical College, Arthur Ashe Jr. Campus, Fort Lauderdale, FL

Angela Kosmas
City Colleges of Chicago, Chicago, IL

John Kruse
University of Maryland, Arnold, MD

Neskys Liriano
New York Mets, Port Saint Lucie, FL

Maria Manikoth
Evergreen Goodwill Job Training and Education Center, Everett, WA

Sean McCroskey
Goodwill, King County, Seattle, WA

Yvonne McMahon
Houston Community College, Houston, TX

Xavier Munoz
Literacy Council of Northern Virginia, Falls Church, VA

Sarah Moussavi
Chaffey College, Rancho Cucamonga, CA

Luba Nesterova
Bilingual Education Institute, Houston, TX

Melody Nguyen
Tarrant County College, Arlington, TX

Joseph Ntumba
Goodwill, King County, Seattle, WA

Sachiko Oates
Santa Barbara City College, Santa Barbara, CA

Liane Okamitsu
McKinley Community School for Adults, Honolulu, HI

Dana Orozco
Sweetwater Union High School District, Chula Vista, CA

Betty Osako
McKinley School For Adults, HI

Dr. Sergei Paromchik
Adult Education Hillsborough County Public Schools, Miami, FL

Ileana Perez
Robert Morgan Tech. College, Miami, FL

Carina Raetz
Academy School District 20, Colorado Springs, CO

Tom Randolph
Notre Dame Education Center, Lawrence, MA

Jody Roy
Notre Dame Education Center, Lawrence, MA

Andrew Sansone
Families for Literacy, Saint Peter's University, Jersey City, NJ

Lea Schultz
Lompoc Adult School and Career Center, Lompoc, CA

Jenny Siegfried
Waubonsee Community College, Aurora, IL

Daina Smudrins
Shoreline Community College, Shoreline, WA

Stephanie Sommers
Minneapolis Adult Education, Robbinsdale, MN

Bonnie Taylor
Genesis Center, RI

Yinebeb T. Tessema
Goodwill, King County, Seattle, WA

Dr. Jacqueline Torres
South Dade Senior High, Homestead, FL

Cristina Urena
Atlantic Technical College, Coconut Creek, FL

Marcos Valle
Edmonds College, Lynnwood, WA

Ricardo Vieira Stanton
Bilingual Education Institute, Houston, TX

Lauren Wilson
Shoreline Community College, Shoreline, WA

Pamela Wilson
Palm Beach County Adult and Community Education, FL

From the Authors

ROB JENKINS

STACI JOHNSON

We believe that there's nothing more incredible than the exchange of teaching and learning that goes on in an ESL classroom. And seeing the expression on a student's face when the light goes on reminds us that there's nothing more rewarding than helping a student succeed.

Throughout our careers, we have watched as students rise to challenges and succeed where they were not sure success was possible. Seeing their confidence grow and skills develop brings great joy to both of us and it motivates us to find better ways to reach and support them. We are humbled to think that our contributions to the field over the last 20 years have made a small difference in both students and teachers' lives. We hope our refinements in ongoing editions will further support their growth and success.

At its core, **Stand Out** has always prioritized robust, relevant content that will deliver student gains in the classroom; while that core mission has not changed, how the program achieves it has certainly evolved in response to changing educational landscape. The basic principles that have made **Stand Out** successful have not changed. Students are challenged to collaborate and think critically through a well-organized series of scaffolded activities that lead to student application in each lesson. The popular first-of-their-kind lesson plans are still prominent. Features such as project-based learning, video, online workbooks, multilevel worksheets, and classroom presentation tools continue to support the core series. New to the fourth edition is explicit workplace exploration. A lesson in each unit has been added to explore different fields and careers, potential salaries, skills, and characteristics which workers might have to excel in potential jobs. Also new to the fourth edition, students will be introduced to *Life Online* in tips, activities, and video throughout the series. In addition, **Stand Out** will now be available in different digital formats compatible with different devices. Finally, **Stand Out** introduces a literacy level that will give access through a unique systematic approach to students who struggle to participate. We believe that with these innovations and features the fourth edition will bring success to every student.

STAND OUT MISSION STATEMENT

Our goal is to inspire students through challenging opportunities to be successful in their language learning experience, so they develop confidence and become independent lifelong learners preparing them for work, school, and life.

Scope and Sequence

UNIT	LESSON 1	LESSON 2	LESSON 3
PRE-UNIT **Welcome** *Page 2*	**Goal:** Greet people and describe feelings **Pronunciation:** /m/ **Grammar:** The Verb *Be*	**Goal:** Complete a registration form **Academic:** Focused listening **Grammar:** Possessive Adjectives	**Goal:** Give and follow instructions **Academic:** Make predictions **Grammar:** Questions with *Can* **Pronunciation:** Yes/No questions intonation **Writing:** Dictation
1 **Everyday Life** *Page 12*	**Goal:** Ask for and give personal information **Pronunciation:** Question intonation **Grammar:** Simple present: *Live* and *Be* **Academic:** Focused listening	**Goal:** Identify family relationships **Grammar:** Simple present: *Have* **Academic:** Make bar graphs	**Goal:** Describe people **Writing:** Write descriptions **Grammar:** Comparative and superlative adjectives **Academic:** Compare
2 **Let's Go Shopping!** *Page 38*	**Goal:** Identify clothing **Academic:** Make predictions; Classify information **Grammar:** Simple present; Negative simple present	**Goal:** Ask about prices **Grammar:** Comparative and Superlative Adjectives **Academic:** Focused listening **Life Online:** Sales Tax	**Goal:** Describe clothing **Grammar:** Present continuous **Writing:** Write descriptions

LESSON 4	LESSON 5	LESSON 6	TEAM PROJECT	READING CHALLENGE
Goal: Interpret and write schedules **Academic:** Make predictions; Interpret schedules **Life Online:** Online calendars **Grammar:** Simple Present	**Goal:** Interpret information about weather **Academic:** Focused listening; Read maps **Life Online:** Severe weather preparedness	**Workforce Goal:** Reflect on career options **Academic:** Read and interpret infographics	**Goal:** Describe a student **Soft Skill:** Collaboration—Sharing Ideas and Brainstorming	*A Shrinking Population* **Academic:** Infer meaning
Goal: Read advertisements and receipts **Academic:** Make predictions; Calculate; Read charts and graphs **Life Online:** Online offers	**Goal:** Ask for assistance **Grammar:** *This, that, these, those* **Academic:** Focused listening	**Workforce Goal:** Identify employment opportunities in the gig economy **Academic:** Interpret infographics; Research	**Goal:** Design a clothing store **Soft Skill:** Collaboration—Coordinating with Others	*What Do Your Clothes Say about You?* **Academic:** Identify main ideas; Infer meaning

Scope and Sequence

UNIT	LESSON 1	LESSON 2	LESSON 3
3 **Food and Nutrition** *Page 64*	**Goal:** Read a menu **Academic:** Make predictions; Calculate; Take notes **Grammar:** Questions with *can*	**Goal:** Make a shopping list **Pronunciation:** Plurals **Grammar:** *Some, any*; Count and noncount nouns: *Much, many* **Academic:** Make predictions; Focused listening	**Goal:** Locate items in a supermarket **Pronunciation:** Rhythm **Academic:** Classify information; Make predictions; Brainstorm ideas **Grammar Review:** The Verb *Be* **Life Online:** Grocery shopping online
4 **Housing** *Page 90*	**Goal:** Describe housing **Grammar:** Information questions and answers **Pronunciation:** Stress and rhythm **Academic:** Make predictions; Make pie charts	**Goal:** Interpret classified ads **Academic:** Do a survey; Focused listening; Classify information	**Goal:** Complete a rental application form **Academic:** Make predictions; Focused listening **Grammar Review:** Information questions **Life Online:** Scams

Life Online Video *Page 116*

5 **Our Community** *Page 118*	**Goal:** Describe your community **Grammar Review:** Information questions **Academic:** Read maps; Classify information	**Goal:** Scan websites and search results **Grammar Review:** Simple present **Academic:** Interpret charts; Focused listening	**Goal:** Give and follow directions **Academic:** Read maps **Grammar:** Imperatives **Writing:** Write directions **Life Online:** Map apps

LESSON 4	LESSON 5	LESSON 6	TEAM PROJECT	READING CHALLENGE
Goal: Identify healthy foods **Grammar Review:** Simple past: *Had/Ate* **Academic:** Classify and rank information; Use Venn diagrams	**Goal:** Read recipes **Grammar:** *How much? / How many?*; Imperatives; Negative imperatives **Academic:** Sequencing; Focused listening	**Workforce Goal:** Identify food-related career options **Academic:** Interpret a donut chart; Classify information	**Goal:** Plan a menu **Soft Skill:** Active Listening —Effective Communication	*Healthy Choices vs. Budgets* **Academic:** Identify topic sentences and main ideas
Goal: Identify rooms and furniture **Academic:** Interpret visuals; Calculate **Grammar Review:** Prepositions of location	**Goal:** Make a family budget **Academic:** Make predictions; Calculate **Grammar:** Modal: *Might*	**Workforce Goal:** Explore construction-related job opportunities **Academic:** Interpret data from infographics	**Goal:** Plan a move **Soft Skill:** Collaboration— Time Management	*Helping Neighbors* **Academic:** Define unknown words; Identify supporting ideas
Goal: Read a message or letter **Life Online:** Attachments **Grammar:** Present continuous **Academic:** Make inferences and predictions **Writing:** Write an email	**Goal:** Write and send a letter or email **Academic:** Sequence **Grammar:** Simple past: Regular and irregular verbs	**Workforce Goal:** Identify employment in public safety careers **Academic:** Make inferences	**Goal:** Describe your community **Skill Focus:** Presentation Skills— Presentation Rubric	*Building Community in Hillsboro* **Academic:** Make inferences; Cite evidence

Scope and Sequence

UNIT	LESSON 1	LESSON 2	LESSON 3
6 **A Healthy Life** *Page 144*	**Goal:** Describe healthy practices **Academic:** Do a survey; Make predictions **Grammar:** Infinitives	**Goal:** Identify illnesses **Academic:** Classify information **Grammar:** Comparative and superlative adjectives	**Goal:** Make a doctor's appointment **Grammar:** Simple past (*be*, regular and irregular verbs) **Academic:** Make predictions **Life Online:** Health information privacy
7 **Work, Work, Work** *Page 170*	**Goal:** Evaluate learning and work skills **Academic:** Focused listening **Grammar:** Future: *Will* (affirmative, negative) **Writing:** Write goals	**Goal:** Identify jobs and job skills **Academic:** Classify information **Grammar:** *Can, can't*	**Goal:** Apply for a job **Pronunciation:** Stress **Academic:** Scan text; Focused listening **Life Online:** Social Security Number
8 **Goals and Lifelong Learning** *Page 196*	**Goal:** Identify goals **Academic:** Focused listening **Grammar:** Future plans: *Hope to, want to, plan to, be going to*	**Goal:** Set academic goals **Academic:** Interpret pie charts **Grammar:** *Because* **Life Online:** Online classes	**Goal:** Set work goals **Academic:** Interpret timelines and Venn diagrams **Grammar:** Future: *Will, be going to*

Life Online Video *Page 222*

	LESSON 4	**LESSON 5**	**LESSON 6**	**TEAM PROJECT**	**READING CHALLENGE**
	Goal: Read medicine labels **Grammar:** Modal: *should* **Academic:** Focused listening	**Goal:** Identify and describe emergencies **Academic:** Read pie charts **Grammar Review:** Simple past (irregular) **Civics:** 911 calls	**Workforce Goal:** Explore careers in the medical field **Academic:** Analyze graphs; Focused listening	**Goal:** Make a health pamphlet **Soft Skill:** Active Listening—Giving Feedback	*A Dangerous Passion* **Academic:** Skimming; Make inferences; Read for details
	Goal: Interview for a job **Life Online:** Virtual interviews **Grammar:** Negative simple past	**Goal:** Follow instructions in an office **Academic:** Sequence **Grammar:** Imperatives	**Workforce Goal:** Compare and contrast jobs in business administration **Academic:** Read infographics	**Goal:** Make your own company **Soft Skill:** Active listening—Asking for Clarification	*Hard Work or Passion?* **Academic:** Reading comprehension
	Goal: Solve problems **Academic:** Make predictions **Grammar:** *Because, so*	**Goal:** Write down goals **Academic:** Make inferences; Focused listening; Make a Venn diagram **Writing:** Format of a paragraph	**Workforce Goal:** Explore employment opportunities in education **Academic:** Read maps and charts	**Goal:** Make a timeline **Soft Skill:** Presentation Skills—Use Technology for Presentations	*The Right to an Education* **Academic:** Identify supporting evidence

Appendices

Life Skills Video Practice 224

Vocabulary List 228

Grammar Reference 230

Skills Index 239

Unit Walkthrough

NEW AND UPDATED IN STAND OUT, FOURTH EDITION

Now in its fourth edition, *Stand Out* is a seven-level, standards-based adult education program with a track record of real-world results. Close alignment to WIOA objectives and College and Career Readiness Standards provides adult students with language and skills for success in the workplace, college, and everyday life.

New Literacy level

**The Literacy level follows an instructional design that meets the needs of lower-level English learners.

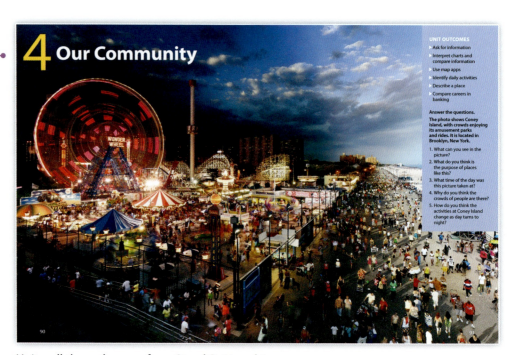

Each unit opens with a dynamic image to introduce the theme and engage learners in meaningful conversations from the start.

Unit walkthrough pages from *Stand Out* Level 3.

xii WELCOME TO STAND OUT

New 'Life Online' sections develop digital literacy skills.

An **updated video program** now features two 'Life Online' videos with related practice that aligns with workforce and digital literacy objectives.

Digital literacy reinforces best practices around privacy, security, finances, and social media.

Unit walkthrough pages from *Stand Out* Level 3.

WELCOME TO *STAND OUT*   xiii

Unit Walkthrough

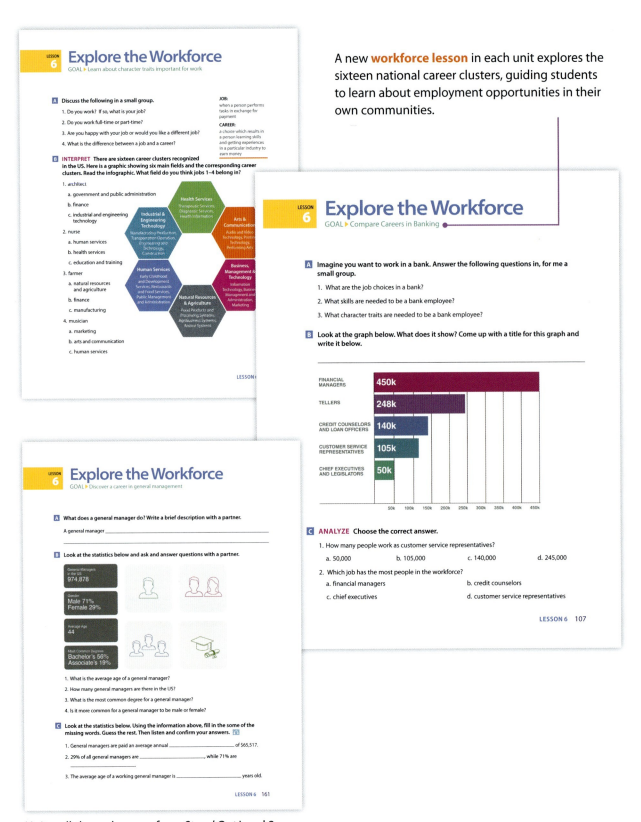

A new **workforce lesson** in each unit explores the sixteen national career clusters, guiding students to learn about employment opportunities in their own communities.

Unit walkthrough pages from *Stand Out* Level 3.

Team Project

Create a Community Brochure
SOFT SKILL ▶ Active Listening

Imagine that a new family has moved into your neighborhood and you want to tell them all about your community. With your team, create a brochure about your community.

1. Form a team with four or five students. Choose a position for each member of your team.

Position	Job Description	Student Name(s)
Student 1: Leader	Check that everyone speaks English. Check that everyone participates.	
Student 2: Writer	Write information for brochure with help from the team.	
Student 3: Designer	Design brochure layout and add artwork.	
Students 4/5: City Representatives	Help writer and designer with their work.	

2. Make a list of everything you want to include in your brochure, for example: information about the library, banks, and other local services.
3. Create the text for your community brochure.
4. Create a map of your community. Then create artwork for your community brochure.
5. Present your brochure to the class.

Active Listening
Listen carefully
Listen carefully while each team is presenting. How is their presentation different than yours? How is it the same?

Public sculptures, like The Bean in Chicago, are great places for people to meet in towns and cities.

TEAM PROJECT 113

Team projects now highlight transferrable **Soft Skills**, such as collaboration, active listening, and presentation skills.

The fully updated **Reading Challenge** will expose students to CASAS STEPS test question types.

Reading Challenge

A PREDICT Look at the company's logo in the photo. What do you think it is a picture of? What types of food and drink do you think they serve at this café?

B Match the vocabulary word to its correct meaning.

____ 1. brunch   a. money that a person gets if he or she loses his or her job
____ 2. pandemic   b. evidence that something is true
____ 3. unemployment   c. a meal that combines breakfast and lunch
____ 4. proof   d. a disease that happens to people all over the world

C Read the text.

D SEQUENCE Put the events in the correct order.

____ Carolina collected unemployment.
_1_ Carolina lived in Guatemala City.
____ Carolina lost her job.
____ Carolina worked as a housekeeper.
____ Carolina built her café.
____ Carolina found a chef and business partner.
____ Carolina crossed the border with her mother.
____ Carolina opened Tikal Café.

E On a separate piece of paper, rewrite the sentences in D in the correct order, adding in extra details from the text. Sometimes, change the name Carolina to "she" to avoid too much repetition and add transitions like *such as, then, next,* etc.

EXAMPLE: Carolina lived in Guatemala City. In 2008, she came to the US with her mother. Then...

F EXPAND Imagine you are planning a visit to Brooklyn for brunch. What would you order?

Rising to the Challenge

Tikal Café is a brunch and coffee shop located in Brooklyn, New York. If you go to its website, you will see delicious menu items such as Avocado Toast, Winter Porridge, a Walnut Pesto Quesadilla and Coconut Yogurt. You can drink Matcha, Iced Lavender Lattes, or Cold Brew Coffee. But what you won't see on the website is that the café is owned by an immigrant, Carolina Hernandez from Guatemala.

Carolina is from Guatemala City, Guatemala, and came to the US with her mother in 2008. For over 10 years, she worked two to three jobs so she could save up enough money to open her own business. Sometimes, she worked 18-hour days. She used the money from her housekeeping job to survive and pay her bills. And she used the money from her food serving job to save for her dream.

Unfortunately, when the pandemic hit in 2020, she lost all of her jobs. She was able to collect unemployment, but she wasn't happy. Carolina was a hard worker and wanted to work to earn her money, not sit on the couch and watch Netflix. So, she found a business partner, who is now the chef at the café, and picked out a location close to her home. She started with an empty space and eventually built Tikal Café, a neighborhood spot where locals can come to enjoy a cup of coffee and a delicious meal. From housekeeper to restaurant owner—Carolina is living proof of the American Dream.

Carolina Hernandez's hard work made her dream come true.

READING CHALLENGE 63

62 UNIT 2

Unit walkthrough pages from *Stand Out* Level 3.

WELCOME TO *STAND OUT*   XV

Unit Walkthrough

spark

Bring *Stand Out* to life with the Spark platform — where you can prepare, teach and assess your classes all in one place!

Manage your course and teach great classes with integrated digital teaching and learning tools. Spark brings together everything you need on an all-in-one platform with a single log-in.

Track student and class performance on independent online practice and assessment, including CASAS practice. The Course Gradebook helps you turn information into insights to make the most of valuable classroom time.

Set up classes and roster students quickly and easily on Spark. Seamless integration options and point-of-use support helps you focus on what matters most: student success.

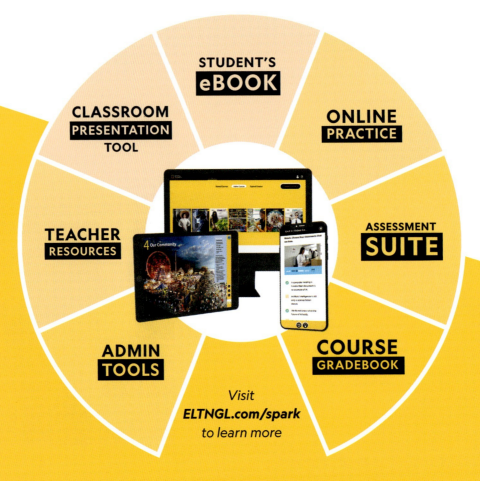

- STUDENT'S eBOOK
- ONLINE PRACTICE
- ASSESSMENT SUITE
- COURSE GRADEBOOK
- ADMIN TOOLS
- TEACHER RESOURCES
- CLASSROOM PRESENTATION TOOL

Visit ELTNGL.com/spark to learn more

CASAS Correlation Chart

PRE-UNIT	Welcome
Lesson 1: Greet people and describe feelings	0.1.1; 0.1.2; 0.1.4, 0.1.5
Lesson 2: Complete a registration form	0.1.2; 0.1.5; 0.2.1; 0.2.2
Lesson 3: Follow instructions	0.1.2; 0.1.5; 0.1.6; 7.5.6

Unit 1	Everyday Life
Lesson 1: Ask for and give personal information	0.1.2; 0.1.5; 0.2.1; 7.5.6
Lesson 2: Identify family relationships	0.1.2; 0.1.5; 0.2.1
Lesson 3: Describe people	0.1.2; 0.1.5; 1.1.4; 4.8.1
Lesson 4: Interpret and write schedules	0.1.2; 0.1.5; 0.2.1; 0.2.4; 2.3.1
Lesson 5: Interpret information about weather	0.1.2; 0.1.5; 2.3.3
Lesson 6: Explore the workforce	0.1.2; 0.1.5; 4.1.3; 4.1.8; 4.8.1, 6.7.3, 7.4.4, 7.7.3
Review	2.3.1, 2.3.2, 2.3.3
Team Project	0.1.2, 0.1.5, 0.2.1, 0.2.4, 2.3.1, 2.3.2, 4.8.1
Reading Challenge	0.1.2, 0.1.5, 4.8.1

Unit 2	Let's Go Shopping!
Lesson 1: Identify clothing	0.1.5; 1.2.9; 4.8.1
Lesson 2: Ask about prices	0.1.2; 0.1.5; 1.1.6, 1.2.1, 1.2.2, 1.3.9
Lesson 3: Describe clothing	0.1.5; 1.1.9, 1.2.9
Lesson 4: Read advertisements and receipts	0.1.2, 0.1.3, 0.1.5; 1.2.1, 1.2.2, 1.2.4, 1.2.9, 4.8.1, 6.7.2
Lesson 5: Ask for Assistance	0.1.2, 0.1.3, 0.1.4, 0.1.5; 1.3.3, 1.2.9
Lesson 6: Explore the workforce	0.1.2, 0.1.5; 4.1.3, 4.1.8, 4.1.9, 4.8.1, 7.4.4, 7.7.3
Review	1.2.9, 1.3.3
Team Project	0.1.2, 0.1.5, 0.2.1, 4.8.1
Reading Challenge	1.2.9, 0.1.5, 4.8.1

Unit 3	Food and Nutrition
Lesson 1: Read a menu	0.1.2, 0.1.5, 1.2.8, 2.6.4
Lesson 2: Make a shopping list	0.1.2, 0.1.5, 1.1.7, 1.2.8
Lesson 3: Locate items in a supermarket	0.1.2, 0.1.5, 1.2.7, 1.2.8, 1.3.1, 7.2.6, 7.3.1
Lesson 4: Identify healthy foods	0.1.2, 0.1.5, 0.2.1, 1.2.8, 3.5.1, 3.5.2, 7.2.3
Lesson 5: Read recipes	0.1.2, 0.1.5, 1.1.1, 1.1.7, 1.2.8
Lesson 6: Explore the workforce	0.1.2, 0.1.5, 4.1.3, 4.1.8, 4.1.9, 4.8.1, 6.7.4, 7.4.4, 7.4.8, 7.7.3
Review	1.1.1, 1.1.7, 1.2.7, 1.2.9, 2.2.1, 2.6.4, 3.5.1, 3.5.2
Team Project	0.1.2, 0.1.5, 1.1.1, 1.1.6, 1.2.4, 1.2.8, 4.8.1
Reading Challenge	0.1.2, 0.1.5, 1.5.2, 3.5.1, 3.5.2

Unit 4	Housing
Lesson 1: Describe housing	0.1.2, 0.1.5, 1.4.1, 1.4.2, 6.7.4
Lesson 2: Interpret classified ads	0.1.2, 0.1.5, 1.4.1, 1.4.2, 7.3.3, 7.4.4
Lesson 3: Complete a rental application	0.1.2, 0.1.5, 1.4.2, 1.4.3, 7.3.3, 7.4.4
Lesson 4: Identify rooms and furniture	0.1.2, 0.1.5, 1.4.1, 1.4.2, 6.1.1, 6.1.3
Lesson 5: Make a family budget	0.1.2, 0.1.5, 1.5.1, 1.8.1, 1.6.1
Lesson 6: Explore careers	0.1.2, 0.1.5, 4.1.3, 4.1.8, 4.1.9, 4.8.1, 7.4.4, 7.4.8, 7.7.3
Review	1.4.1, 1.4.2, 1.4.3, 1.5.1, 6.1.1
Team Project	0.1.2, 0.1.5, 1.4.2, 1.5.1, 4.8.1, 6.1.1, 6.1.3
Reading Challenge	0.1.2, 0.1.5, 4.8.1

Unit 5	Our Community
Lesson 1: Describe your community	0.1.2, 0.1.5, 2.2.4, 2.2.5
Lesson 2: Scan websites and search results	0.1.2, 0.1.5, 2.1.1, 2.4.2, 7.3.4
Lesson 3: Give and follow directions	0.1.2, 0.1.5, 2.2.1, 2.2.5
Lesson 4: Read a message or letter	0.1.2, 0.1.5, 0.2.3
Lesson 5: Write and send a letter	0.1.2, 0.1.5, 0.2.3
Lesson 6: Explore the Workforce	0.1.2, 0.1.5, 4.1.3, 4.1.8, 4.1.9, 4.8.1, 6.7.2, 7.4.4, 7.7.3
Review	0.2.3, 2.2.5, 2.4.2
Team Project	0.1.2, 0.1.5, 0.2.3, 2.2.1, 2.2.5, 4.8.1
Reading Challenge	0.1.2, 0.1.5, 2.5.8, 4.8.1

Unit 6	Health and Fitness
Lesson 1: Describe healthy practices	0.1.2, 0.1.5, 3.5.7, 3.5.9
Lesson 2: Identify illnesses	0.1.2, 0.1.5, 3.6.3
Lesson 3: Make a doctor's appointment	0.1.2, 0.1.5, 3.6.4
Lesson 4: Read medicine labels	0.1.2, 0.1.5, 3.3.1, 3.3.2, 3.4.1
Lesson 5: Identify and describe emergencies	0.1.2, 0.1.5, 2.1.2, 2.5.1, 6.6.5, 6.7.4
Lesson 6: Explore the Workforce	0.1.2, 0.1.5, 4.1.3, 4.1.8, 4.1.9, 4.4.3, 4.8.1, 6.6.5, 6.7.3, 7.4.4, 7.7.3
Review	3.6.1, 3.6.3
Team Project	0.1.2, 0.1.5, 3.3.2, 3.3.4, 3.6.3, 4.8.1
Reading Challenge	0.1.2, 0.1.5, 2.5.1

Unit 7	Working on It
Lesson 1: Evaluate learning and work skills	0.1.2, 0.1.5, 4.4.1, 4.4.2, 4.7.3
Lesson 2: Identify jobs and job skills	0.1.2, 0.1.5, 4.1.2, 4.1.8, 4.5.1
Lesson 3: Apply for a job	0.1.2, 0.1.5, 4.1.1, 4.1.2, 4.1.3, 4.1.6, 7.4.4, 7.7.3
Lesson 4: Interview for a job	0.1.2, 0.1.5, 4.1.5, 4.1.7
Lesson 5: Follow instructions in an office	0.1.2, 0.1.5, 1.7.3, 4.6.1
Lesson 6: Compare and contrast jobs in business administration	0.1.2, 0.1.5, 4.1.3, 4.1.8, 4.1.9, 4.4.3, 6.6.5, 7.4.4, 7.7.3
Review	4.1.2, 4.1.3, 4.1.5, 4.1.6, 4.1.7, 4.1.8, 4.4.1, 4.4.2, 4.5.1, 4.6.1, 4.7.3
Team Project	0.1.2, 0.1.5, 4.1.1, 4.1.2, 4.1.3, 4.1.5, 4.1.6, 4.8.1
Reading Challenge	0.1.2, 0.1.5, 4.1.2, 4.1.9

Unit 8	Goals and Lifelong Learning
Lesson 1: Identify goals	0.1.2, 0.1.5, 4.4.5, 7.1.1, 7.5.1
Lesson 2: Set academic goals	0.1.2, 0.1.5, 6.7.4, 7.1.1, 7.2.3, 7.5.1
Lesson 3: Set work goals	0.1.2, 0.1.5, 4.4.5, 6.6.5, 7.1.1, 7.1.2, 7.2.3
Lesson 4: Find ways to learn	0.1.2, 0.1.5, 2.5.6, 7.2.7, 7.3.1, 7.3.2, 7.5.5
Lesson 5: Record goals	0.1.2, 0.1.5, 4.4.5, 6.6.5, 7.1.1, 7.1.2
Lesson 6: Explore careers	0.1.2, 0.1.5, 4.1.3, 4.1.8, 4.1.9, 7.4.4, 7.7.3
Review	4.4.5, 7.1.1, 7.1.2, 7.1.3, 7.5.1
Team Project	0.1.2, 0.1.5, 4.4.5, 4.8.1, 7.1.1, 7.1.2, 7.1.3, 7.5.1
Reading Challenge	0.1.2, 0.1.5, 7.1.1, 7.1.2, 7.1.3, 7.5.1

For more correlations, including ELPS, CCRS, and ELCivics, visit the Spark Platform.

PRE-UNIT
Welcome

UNIT OUTCOMES
- Greet people and describe feelings
- Complete a registration form
- Give and follow instructions

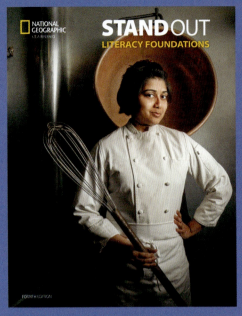

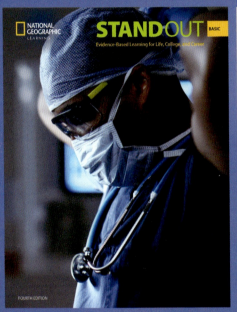
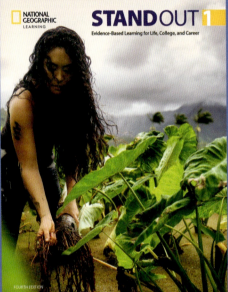

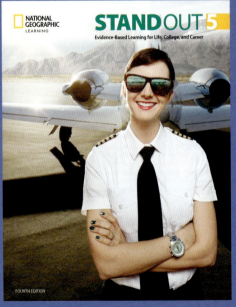

LESSON 1

Nice to Meet You!

GOAL ▶ Greet people and describe feelings

A PREDICT The teacher is greeting the student. What are they saying?

B Listen to Lien and Mario. Who is the new student? Practice the conversation.

Mario: Hello, what's your name?
Lien: My name is Lien.
Mario: Nice to meet you, Lien. I'm Mario.
Lien: Hi, Mario. Nice to meet you, too.
Mario: Welcome to our class, Lien.

C Listen to the conversations. Choose the new student.

1. Mario   (Lien)   2. Esteban   Suma
3. Asad   Li   4. Nadia   Abdul

D Look at the photos. Say the words.

nervous

sad

tired

happy

angry

frustrated

E Listen and repeat.

I'm nervous. We have a test.

I'm so sad. My friend isn't coming.

I'm tired. I didn't get very much sleep last night.

I'm happy. It's Friday!

I'm a little angry.

I'm frustrated because this is difficult.

F Practice the conversations.

Mario: Hi, Lien!
Lien: Hello, Mario.
Mario: How are you today?
Lien: I'm <u>nervous</u>. We have a test.
Mario: Me too.

Li: Hi, Asad!
Asad: Hello, Li.
Li: How are you today?
Asad: I'm <u>sad</u>. My friend isn't coming.
Li: Oh, I'm sorry.

G Practice the conversations in F with a partner. Use different feelings.

4   PRE-UNIT

H Study the chart with your classmates and teacher.

The Verb *Be*			
Subject	*Be*	Feelings	Example Sentence
I	am	fine	I **am** fine. (I**'m** fine.)
You / We / They	are	nervous	You **are** nervous. (You**'re** nervous.)
		sad	We **are** sad. (We**'re** sad.)
		tired	They **are** tired. (They**'re** tired.)
He / She / It	is	angry	He **is** angry. (He**'s** angry.)
		frustrated	She **is** frustrated. (She**'s** frustrated.)
NOTE: Contractions are more common when speaking, but they can be used in informal writing.			

I Complete the sentences with the correct form of the verb *be*.

1. Mauricio _____ tired today.
2. They _____ hungry.
3. Antonio and I _____ angry.
4. I _____ fine, thank you.
5. Alice _____ nervous.
6. You _____ happy.

J **SURVEY** Ask classmates how they are feeling. Write their answers.

Student Name	Feelings (How are you today?)
Mario	happy

K Work in a group. Talk about your conversations.

EXAMPLE: Mario's happy.

LESSON 1

LESSON 2

What's Your Name and Number?

GOAL ▶ Complete a registration form

A **INTERPRET** Read the school registration form. Look up any new words in a dictionary.

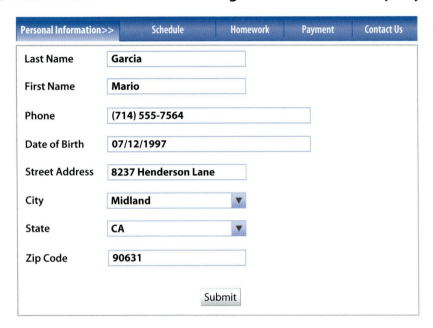

B Complete the sentences.

1. Mario's last name is _____.
2. His phone number is _____.
3. His address is _____.
4. His zip code is _____.
5. His date of birth is _____.

C Listen and write the information you hear. 🎧

1. His first name is _____.
2. His last name is _____.
3. He lives on _____. (street address)
4. He lives in _____. (city)
5. He's from _____.
6. His teacher's last name is _____.

6 PRE-UNIT

D Listen. Practice saying the numbers.

0	1	2	3	4	5	6	7	8	9
10	11	12	13	14	15	16	17	18	19
20	21	22	23	24	25	26	27	28	29
30	40	50	60	70	80	90	100		

E Listen. Write the phone numbers.

1. (619) 555-6391
2. _____
3. _____
4. _____
5. _____
6. _____

F Listen to the conversations. Write the missing information.

1. My name is Marie. I live in Palm City. I go to West Palm Adult School. My phone number is _____. My last name is Collell.

2. My name is Aung. I live in Boyle Heights. My address is _____ Third Street.

3. My name is Luis. It's nice to meet you. My phone number is _____.

Two friends exchange phone numbers.

G Study the chart with your classmates and teacher.

Possessive Adjectives		
Pronoun	Possessive Adjective	Example Sentence
I	My	**My** address is 3356 Archer Boulevard.
You	Your	**Your** phone number is (123) 555-5678.
He	His	**His** last name is Yang.
She	Her	**Her** first name is Lien.
It	Its	**Its** number is 10.
We	Our	**Our** teacher is Mr. Kelley.
They	Their	**Their** home is in Minneapolis.

H Complete each sentence with a possessive adjective.

1. I live in San Francisco. _____ address is 2354 Yerba Buena.

2. They live in Portland. _____ phone number is (971) 555-6732.

3. We live in Dallas. _____ last name is Peters.

4. Maria is a happy woman. _____ school is in New York.

5. He is a good student. _____ name is Esteban Gomez.

6. You live on Hilton Street. _____ home is in Rockledge. Is that right?

7. She lives on a big road. _____ name is Charles Road.

I **APPLY** Talk to a partner. Complete the form with your partner's information.

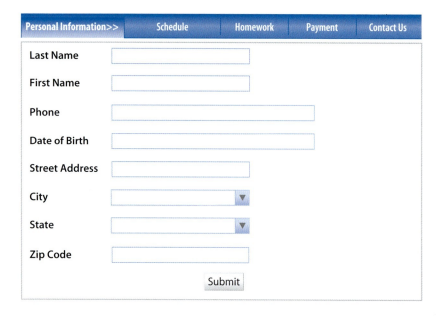

8 PRE-UNIT

LESSON 3

Open Your Books!
GOAL ▶ Give and follow instructions

A Match the instructions with the photos. Write the correct sentence under each photo.

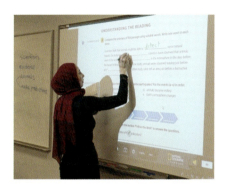

1. _____

2. _____

3. _____

4. _____

| Go to the board. | Open the book. | Talk to a partner. | Write the answer. |

B Work with a partner. Choose the words that describe classroom activities.

(answer)	ride	take out
eat	run	talk
listen	sit down	watch
open	sleep	work
practice	stand up	write

LESSON 3   9

C PREDICT Look at the photo. What's wrong with the student?

D Read and listen to the conversation.

Mr. Jones: Alicia, <u>please write a sentence on the board</u>.
Alicia: <u>Excuse me</u>?
Mr. Jones: <u>Write a sentence on the board</u>.
Alicia: <u>I'm sorry, I don't understand</u>.
Mr. Jones: I can help you.
Alicia: OK.

Life ONLINE

🖐 In an online class, make sure you raise your hand when you need to ask for clarification. You can also write your questions in the chat.

E Study the phrases with your classmates and teacher.

I'm sorry, I don't understand.	Excuse me?
Please speak slower.	Can you say that again, please?
Please speak louder.	Can you spell that?

F Look at **D** again. Make new conversations with the classroom instructions.

1. Please stand up and walk to the door. Then return.
2. Please write my name on a piece of paper.
3. Please ask the teacher for a pencil.

10   PRE-UNIT

G Study the chart with your classmates and teacher.

Questions with *Can*			
Can	Pronoun	Verb	Example Sentence
Can	you	help speak answer repeat say spell	Can you help me? Can you speak slower? Can you answer the question? Can you repeat that, please? Can you say it again, please? Can you spell it, please?

Yes/No Questions

When we ask questions that have a *yes* or *no* answer, we raise the pitch of our voice on the last syllable of the sentence. Try reading the six questions in the grammar chart out loud.

Can you help me?

Can you speak slower?

H **CLARIFY** Complete the conversation with questions from **G**. Then practice the conversation with a partner.

Student A: I have a problem. *Can you help me?* _____

Student B: Sure.

Student A: Your name is difficult to spell. _____

Student B: Yes, it is R-O-X-A-N-N-A.

Student A: You speak very fast. _____

Student B: Yes, of course. It's R-O-X-A-N-N-A.

Student A: Thanks!

I Listen. Write the instructions.

1. _____

2. _____

3. _____

4. _____

5. _____

6. _____

LESSON 3

1 Everyday Life

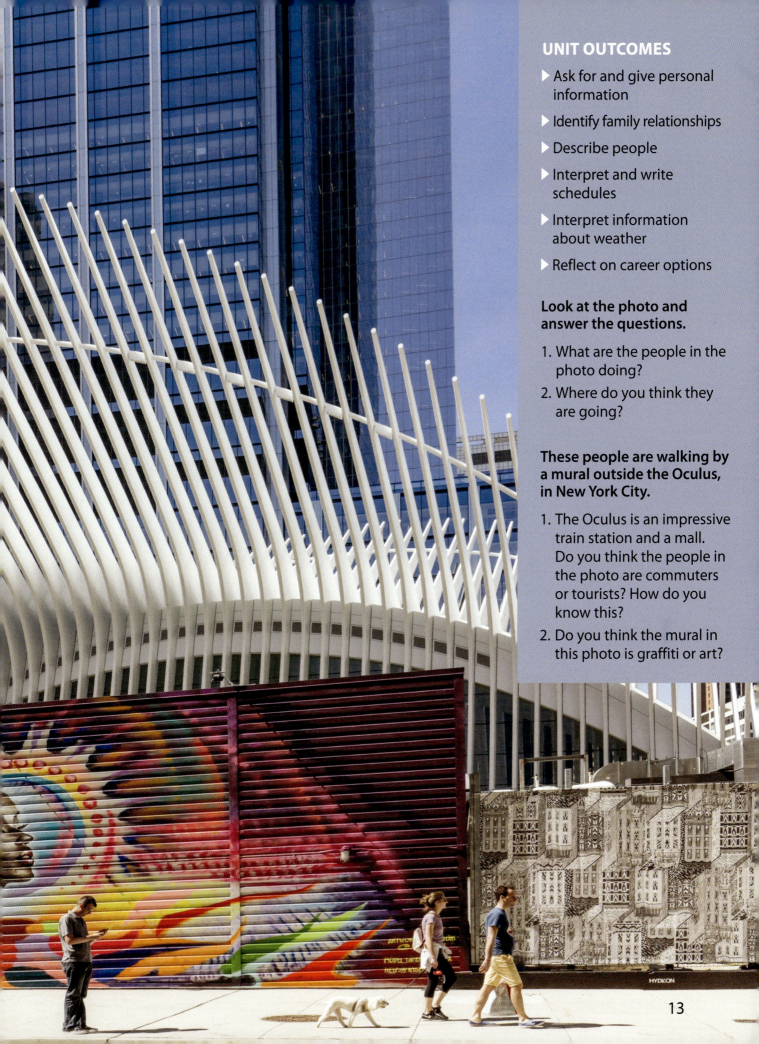

UNIT OUTCOMES

▸ Ask for and give personal information

▸ Identify family relationships

▸ Describe people

▸ Interpret and write schedules

▸ Interpret information about weather

▸ Reflect on career options

Look at the photo and answer the questions.

1. What are the people in the photo doing?
2. Where do you think they are going?

These people are walking by a mural outside the Oculus, in New York City.

1. The Oculus is an impressive train station and a mall. Do you think the people in the photo are commuters or tourists? How do you know this?
2. Do you think the mural in this photo is graffiti or art?

LESSON 1

Where Are You From?

GOAL ▶ Ask for and give personal information

A Look at the map. Find and point to your country.

B Look at **A**. Complete the sentences. Then ask a partner where he or she is from. Write his or her answer.

1. Grace is from _____, Nigeria.

   She lives in _____.

2. Sima is from _____, Afghanistan.

   She lives in _____.

3. Gilberto is from _____, Brazil.

   He lives in _____.

4. I am from _____.

   I live in _____.

5. My partner is from _____.

   My partner lives in _____.

14   UNIT 1

C CLASSIFY Read the words in the box and complete the table.

25 years old	divorced	single
city	married	state
~~country~~	old	young

Marital Status	Age	Place
		country

D Listen to the conversation. Then use the information to make new conversations.

Grace
Single
20 years old
Lagos, Nigeria

Sima
Married
26 years old
Kabul, Afghanistan

Gilberto
Single
30 years old
Rio de Janeiro, Brazil

Marie
Divorced
45 years old
Port-au-Prince, Haiti

Gilberto: Where is Grace from?

Marie: She's from Nigeria.

Gilberto: How old is she?

Marie: She's 20 years old.

Gilberto: Is she married?

Marie: No, she's single.

Question Intonation

Yes / No questions have rising intonation.

Is she married?

Information questions have falling intonation.

Where is Grace from?

E Study the charts with your classmates and teacher.

Simple Present: *Live*			
Subject	Verb	Information	Example Sentence
I / We / You / They	live	in Los Angeles in California in the United States	I **live** in Los Angeles. You **live** in Los Angeles, California.
He / She / It	lives		He **lives** in the United States. She **lives** in Mexico.

Simple Present: *Be*			
Subject	Verb	Information	Example Sentence
I	am	from Vietnam	I **am** from Vietnam.
We / You / They	are	single divorced	We **are** single. You **are** divorced.
He / She / It	is	23 years old	He **is** 23 years old. She **is** 23 years old.

F Write the correct verb for each sentence. Then listen and complete.

1. Lien _____ from Ho Chi Minh City, _____.
2. She _____ _____ years old.
3. She _____ in _____.
4. Mario _____ _____ years old.
5. He also _____ in _____.
6. He _____ from _____.
7. Mario and Lien are not married. They _____.

G **SURVEY** Ask classmates for personal information and write sentences. Then share the information with the class.

EXAMPLE: Student A: Where do you live?
Student B: I live in Chicago.

LESSON 2

Manny's Family

GOAL ▶ Identify family relationships

A INTERPRET Read and listen to Manny's story. How many people are in his family?

> My name is Manuel Perez. My friends call me Manny. I have a wonderful family. We live in the United States. I have one sister and two brothers. I also have uncles and an aunt here. My father has two brothers and no sisters. My mother has one brother and one sister. My parents are in Venezuela. I'm sad because they are not here with the rest of my family.

B Read Manny's story again and complete the sentences.

1. Manny has _____ sister.

2. Manny has _____ brothers.

3. Manny's father has _____ brothers and _____ sisters.

4. Manny's mother has _____ sister and _____ brother.

C Study Manny's family tree. Who lives in Venezuela?

LESSON 2   17

D Study the words with your classmates and teacher.

parents	daughter	aunt	grandchildren
father	son	uncle	grandfather
mother	brother	niece	grandmother
husband	sister	nephew	grandson
wife		cousin	granddaughter

E Look at the family tree in **C**. Write the correct words under each picture.

1.
   grandfather / _granddaughter_

2.
   _____ / _____

3.
   _____ / _____

4.
   _____ / _____

5.
   _____ / _____

6.
   _____ / _____

F Ask and answer questions about the people in **E**.

EXAMPLE: **Student A:** How are Pedro and Carmen related?
Student B: They are grandfather and granddaughter.

These are some other words you can use to talk about your family: partner, spouse, stepsister, half-brother.

G Study the chart with your classmates and teacher.

Simple Present: Have			
Subject	**Verb**	**Information**	**Example Sentence**
I / You / We / They	have	three brothers two sisters	I **have** three brothers. You **have** two sisters.
He / She / It	has	no cousins three sons	He **has** no cousins. She **has** three sons.

H Listen. Choose the correct form of *have* and write the missing information.

1. Thanh have / has _____ sisters.

2. I have / has _____ brothers.

3. Ricardo and Patty have / has _____ children.

4. Orlando, you have / has _____ cousins.

5. Maria have / has _____ sisters.

6. We have / has _____ child.

I **APPLY** Complete the chart. Talk to four classmates about their siblings and children.

siblings: brothers and sisters
stepbrother / stepsister: your parent's spouse's child

EXAMPLE: You: How many siblings and children do you have?

Juan: I have three siblings: two brothers and a stepsister. I have two children.

S: Siblings / C: Children

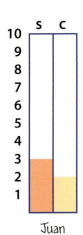
Juan

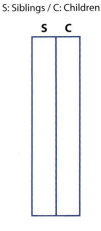

J **CREATE** Make your own family tree and share it with the class.

LESSON 2 19

LESSON 3

Manny's Class
GOAL ▸ Describe people

A Look at Manny's class. Who is tall? Who has blond hair?

Height: short, average height, tall
Weight: thin, average weight, heavy
He **is** tall and average weight.

Eyes: brown, blue, green, gray, hazel
Hair: black, brown, blond, red, gray, white
She **has** brown eyes and black hair.

B Describe four people in **A**.

1a. Dalva is average height and average weight.
2a. He ~~has~~ is brown hair
3a. She is average height and thin
4a. Lien ~~has~~ is tall and thin

1b. Dalva has green eyes and blond hair.
2b. Vera has white hair
3b. Marie has brown eyes
4b. Lien has brown hair

20 UNIT 1

C Listen and complete the chart. Write sentences.

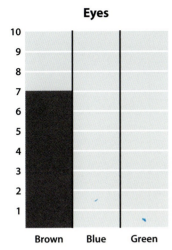

1. Seven people have brown eyes.
2. two people have blue eyes
3. One people have green eyes

D ANALYZE Look at the picture in **A**. In a group, complete the charts.

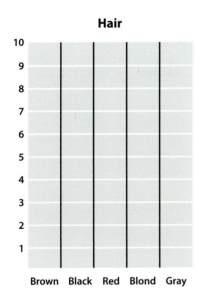
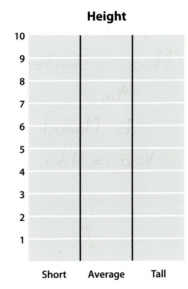
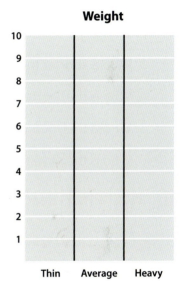

E Work with a partner. Practice the conversation. Then look at **A** and describe a student. Your partner should guess.

EXAMPLE: Student A: He is short and has black hair. Guess who.
                Student B: Mario?
                Student A: Yes, that's right. / No, try again.

F Read the chart with your classmates and teacher.

Comparative and Superlative Adjectives		
Adjective	**Comparative Adjective**	**Superlative Adjective**
tall	taller	the tallest
short	shorter	the shortest
old	older	the oldest
young	younger	the youngest
Use *than* when using comparative adjectives. Henry is taller *than* Karen.		

G **COMPARE** Look at the picture in **A**. Answer the questions in full sentences.

1. Who is taller than Manny? <u>Lien is taller than Manny.</u>
2. Who is the tallest in the class? <u>Ahmed is taller</u>
3. Who is shorter than Dalva? <u>Mario is shorter than dalva</u>
4. Who is the shortest in the class? <u>Mario is shortest</u>
5. Who is the youngest in the class? <u>Is Mahad</u>
6. Who is the oldest in the class? <u>Vera is older</u>

H **INTERPRET** Read the paragraph. Underline the superlative adjectives.

There are thirty students in my class. Twenty-five students have black hair. Five students have brown hair. The tallest student in the class is Francisco. The shortest is Eva. I think the youngest student is Nadia.

I **APPLY** Write a paragraph about your class. Use the paragraph in **H** as a model.

There are thirteen students in my class. Twelve students have black hair and one student has brown hair. The tallest student in the class is Jean Daniel. The shortest is Jennifer and the youngest student is Luis.

LESSON 4 My Schedule

GOAL ▶ Interpret and write schedules

A PREDICT Look at the calendar. Why are the events different colors?

NOVEMBER

SUN	MON	TUE	WED	THU	FRI	SAT
31	1	2 Election Day	3	4 School closes 2 p.m.	5 Meet friends for dinner	6
7	8 School closes 2 p.m.	9	10	11 School closed / Veterans Day	12	13
14 Meet friends for dinner	15	16	17 Mom's birthday	18	19	20
21	22	23 Arnel doctor visit	24	25 Thanksgiving Day	26 School closed	27
28 AM workout class	29 Vacation	30 Vacation	1 Vacation	2 Vacation	3 Vacation	4 Vacation

■ Personal calendar   ■ Family   ■ National holidays

B Read and listen to the conversation. 🎧

Mother: Hi, Gloria.

Gloria: Hi, Mom. I need your help. Can you pick up Arnel? School is closing early today.

Mother: Sure. What time?

Gloria: Two o'clock. It's in the family calendar.

Mother: Okay, no problem. See you when you get home.

C Practice the conversation. Use the information in the calendar to make new conversations.

Online calendars and scheduling applications for mobile devices can be very useful. These tools can help you schedule important appointments and events and set reminders. Some calendars can even be shared with family and friends. Just make sure you schedule your friend's surprise birthday party in your personal calendar and not the shared calendar!

LESSON 4   23

D INTERPRET Read Gilberto's calendar. Then listen and point to the days.

Gilberto's Calendar

SUNDAY	MONDAY	TUESDAY	WEDNESDAY	THURSDAY	FRIDAY	SATURDAY
		1 wake up at 5:00 a.m. go to school work	**2** wake up at 5:00 a.m. go to school work make dinner	**3** wake up at 5:00 a.m. go to school work	**4** wake up at 5:00 a.m. go to school work	**5** wake up at 5:00 a.m. work overtime
6 wake up at 6:00 a.m. play soccer	**7** wake up at 5:00 a.m. go to school work make dinner	**8** wake up at 5:00 a.m. go to school work	**9** wake up at 5:00 a.m. go to school work make dinner	**10** wake up at 5:00 a.m. go to school work	**11** wake up at 5:00 a.m. go to school work	**12** wake up at 5:00 a.m. go to the beach
13 wake up at 6:00 a.m. play soccer	**14** wake up at 5:00 a.m. go to school work make dinner	**15** wake up at 5:00 a.m. go to school work	**16** wake up at 5:00 a.m. go to school work make dinner	**17** wake up at 5:00 a.m. go to school work	**18** wake up at 5:00 a.m. go to school work	**19** wake up at 5:00 a.m. work overtime

E Choose the answers to the questions.

1. What does Gilberto do from Monday to Friday?
    a. He plays with his children.
    b. He works and goes to school.
    c. He plays soccer.

2. What does he do every Monday and Wednesday?
    a. He makes dinner.
    b. He cleans the house.
    c. He wakes up at 7:00 a.m.

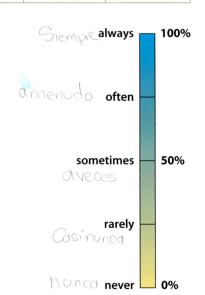

Siempre always — 100%
a menudo often
sometimes — 50%
a veces
rarely
Casi nunca
nunca never — 0%

F Choose *True* or *False* for each sentence.

1. Gilberto sometimes goes to work on Saturday.   True   False
2. He never plays soccer on Sunday.   True   False
3. He always gets up at 5:00 a.m.   True   False
4. He rarely goes to the beach.   True   False

G Study the chart with your classmates and teacher.

Simple Present			
Subject	Verb	Information	Example Sentence
I / You / We / They	eat go make play	lunch to school dinner soccer	I **eat** lunch at twelve o'clock. You **go** to school at 8:00 a.m. We sometimes **make** dinner. They **play** soccer on Saturday.
He / She / It	eats* goes** makes* plays**	lunch to school dinner soccer	He **eats** lunch at twelve o'clock. Nadia **goes** to school at 10:00 a.m. Gilberto **makes** dinner. She **plays** soccer on Friday.
Pronunciation: */s/ **/z/			

H Practice the conversation. Use Gilberto's calendar in **D** to make new conversations.

Student A: What does Gilberto do on Monday?

Student B: He works and goes to school on Monday.

I **APPLY** Work with a partner. Ask: "What do you do in the morning?" Write your partner's schedule. Then report to a group.

5:00 a.m. _____

6:00 a.m. _____

7:00 a.m. _____

8:00 a.m. _____

9:00 a.m. _____

10:00 a.m. _____

11:00 a.m. _____

12:00 p.m. _____

LESSON 5 How Is the Weather Today?

GOAL ▶ Interpret information about weather

A Review the words and icons with your teacher.

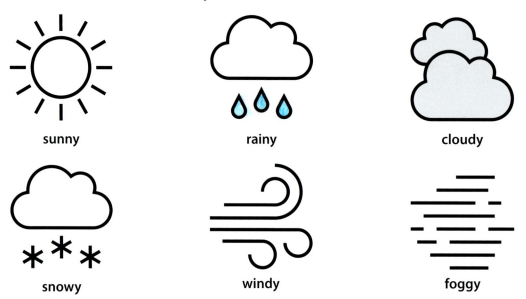

sunny   rainy   cloudy

snowy   windy   foggy

B Listen to the weather report. Write the temperatures on the map.

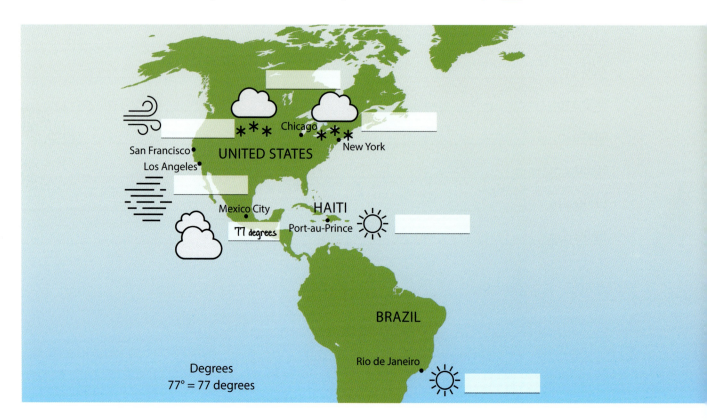

Degrees
77° = 77 degrees

26   UNIT 1

C Work in pairs. Ask your partner questions about the map to complete your chart. Then switch roles.

Student A: How's the weather in Mexico City?
Student B: It's cloudy and 77 degrees.

Student A

City	Weather	Temperature
Mexico City	cloudy	77°
Los Angeles		
New York		
Port-au-Prince		

Student B

City	Weather	Temperature
Lagos		
Kabul		
Ho Chi Minh City		
Rio de Janeiro		

D **RESEARCH** Ask about your partner's country.

Country	Weather	Temperature

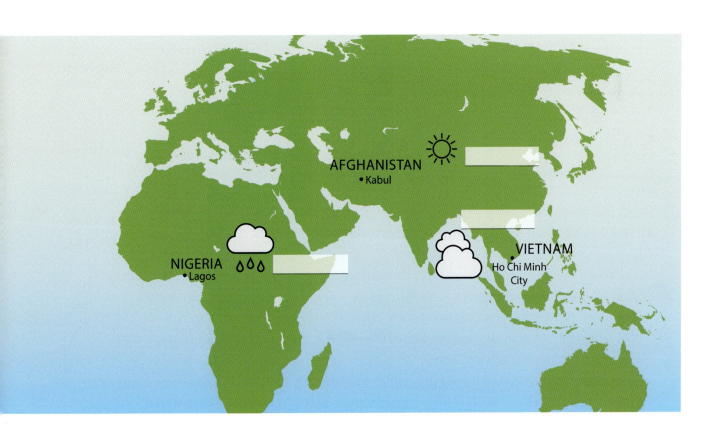

E Write the correct word for each photo. Then discuss your answers with the class.

| blizzard | dust storm | firestorm | flood | hurricane | tornado |

1. _____ 2. _____ 3. _____

4. _____ 5. _____ 6. _____

F Look at the photos in E. Match the words and definitions.

1. _____ blizzard   a. winds that move quickly in the shape of a funnel
2. _____ dust storm   b. storm with winds and rain that starts in the ocean
3. _____ wildfire   c. strong snowstorm with high winds
4. _____ flood   d. overflow of water onto dry land
5. _____ hurricane   e. strong winds that carry dust, sand, and soil
6. _____ tornado   f. large fire that spreads through forests

G Read the text. Then, on a separate piece of paper, make a list of all the devices you need to charge before a severe weather event.

When a severe weather event is in the forecast, you need to be prepared. Charging your devices is now as important as making sure you have enough food and water. If you lose power, you can use your device, like a smartphone or a tablet, to get important information like updates about the weather, power, schools, and travel conditions. Your Wi-Fi will not work, but your device can probably use data from your phone company. Use your device only when you need it for important information and emergencies. When power is restored, make sure to switch your device back to wifi.

28 UNIT 1

LESSON 6
Explore the Workforce
GOAL ▶ Reflect on career options

A Read about careers. Underline the words you think are most important.

> In **Stand Out**, we explore careers in every unit. A career and a job are different. A job is anything we do to earn money. A career is work we do in a *work area* where we continue to progress and learn throughout our lives. The career "areas" are called clusters. The United States identifies career clusters. These clusters are in six different fields.

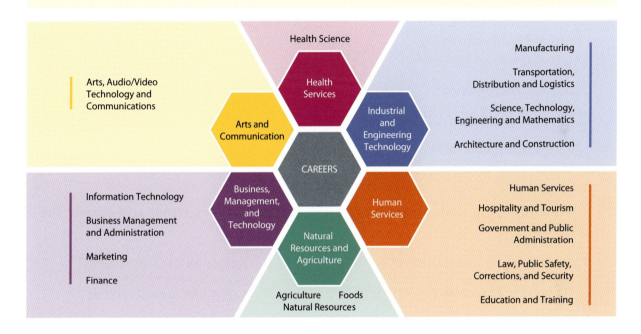

B **INTERPRET** Study the information in **A**. Answer the questions.

1. Which field includes Marketing?

   a. Arts and Communication   b. Human Services   c. Business, Management, and Technology

2. Which field includes Tourism?

   a. Human Services   b. Health Services   c. Arts

3. Which field might include jobs about the environment?

   a. Information Technology   b. Industrial Technology   c. Natural Resources and Agriculture

C Work in a group. Take turns saying which field is interesting to you. Explain why.

D Look at the jobs and complete the chart.

| actor | food scientist | salesperson |
| construction engineer | nurse | social worker |

Career Field	Job	Other Jobs (Look online for more ideas.)
Health Services		
Industrial and Engineering Technology		
Human Services		
Natural Resources and Agriculture		
Business, Management, and Technology		
Arts and Communication		

E Think about your skills and what you like to do. Talk to a partner and answer the questions.

1. Do you like to work outside or inside?
2. Do you like to work with your hands?
3. Do you like to work alone or with others?
4. Do you like to create new things?
5. Do you like to come up with new ideas?
6. Do you like to lead?
7. Do you like to change ideas?
8. Do you like to help others?
9. Do you like to work at a desk or do physical work?
10. Do you like to solve problems?
11. Do you want to make a lot of money?
12. Do you want a fixed or flexible schedule?

F Choose the character traits that describe you. Look up any words you don't know.

motivated	reliable	organized	outgoing	friendly
detail-oriented	tech-savvy	calm	responsible	hardworking
independent	creative	reserved	honest	ambitious

G Discuss the information regarding pay for Veterinary Technologists and Technicians in the United States.

lowest salary:
$28,370

median salary:
$36,850

highest salary:
$48,100

H **INTERPRET** Skim the job ad. Circle the job title, one qualification, and one responsibility.

Animal Care National is looking for an individual to join our team. Our ideal candidate loves animals, is dependable, and is dedicated.

Position: Veterinary Technician

Requirements: Minimum of AA degree or more in animal science or other related field; minimum of one year of experience in veterinary technology and animal care.

Responsibilities

- Perform duties related to care of animals in a laboratory setting
- Maintenance and deep cleaning of all facilities where animals are caged
- Perform noninvasive tests and exams of animals while ensuring animal safety
- Keep accurate records
- Other duties as assigned

Skills

- Basic computer skills
- Ability to problem solve
- Able to work with a team

I **REFLECT** Would you like to be a veterinary technician? Why? Answer the questions in a group.

1. Does this job interest you? Why?

2. Do you think the pay for this type of job is good? How much do you need to make to support yourself and your family?

3. Which skills do you have right now?

4. Do you think after you get experience and education that you could do this job?

J Go online and search for any jobs that interest you. What is the pay? How much education do you need?

Review

A Read the information. Answer the questions in complete sentences.

Jarom
married
72
Latakia, Syria
Residence: California

Elia
single
65
Bogota, Colombia
Residence: California

1. Where is Jarom from?

   He is from _____.

2. Where do Jarom and Elia live?

   They _____.

3. How old is Jarom?

   Jarom _____.

4. Who is older, Jarom or Elia?

   _____

5. Are Jarom and Elia married?

   _____

B Write *live* or *lives*.

1. Gilberto and Lien _____ in Los Angeles.

2. We _____ with our mother and father.

3. I _____ in California.

4. Mario _____ in a house.

5. Eshani _____ in Afghanistan.

6. You _____ in the United States.

Learner Log I can ask for and give personal information.
☐ Yes ☐ No ☐ Maybe

32 UNIT 1

C Look at the family tree and write the relationships.

1. Dimitri and Nadia are _____husband_____ and _____wife_____.
2. Dimitri and Vladimir are _____ and _____.
3. Nadia and Natalya are _____ and _____.
4. Irina and Natalya are _____ and _____.
5. Ivan and Vladimir are _____ and _____.

D Write about Mario in Lesson 3. Describe his height, weight, age, hair, and eyes.

_____
_____
_____
_____
_____
_____

Learner Log

I can identify family relationships.
☐ Yes ☐ No ☐ Maybe

I can describe people.
☐ Yes ☐ No ☐ Maybe

REVIEW 33

Review

E Write the weather words under the pictures.

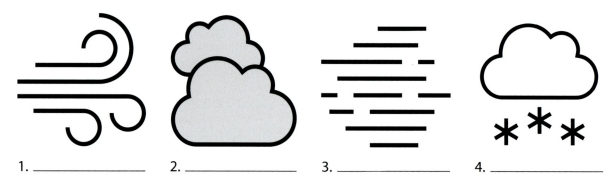

1. _____ 2. _____ 3. _____ 4. _____

F Read Daniela's schedule.

G Describe Daniela's day. Write four complete sentences.

1. _____
2. _____
3. _____
4. _____

Learner Log I can interpret information about weather. ☐ Yes ☐ No ☐ Maybe   I can interpret and write schedules. ☐ Yes ☐ No ☐ Maybe

Team Project

Describe a Student
SOFT SKILL ▶ Collaboration

In this project, you are going to describe a student on your team or a student from the picture in Lesson 3. You will include a family tree, a one-day planner, and a one-month calendar for the student.

1. Form a team with four or five students. In your team, you need:

Position	Job Description	Student Name
Student 1: **Team Leader**	Check that everyone speaks English. Check that everyone participates.	
Student 2: **Writer**	Write a paragraph with help from the team.	
Student 3: **Artist**	Make a family tree with help from the team.	
Students 4 / 5: **Planners**	Make a one-day planner and a one-month calendar with help from the team.	

2. Choose a student from your team or a student from the picture in Lesson 3.

3. Write a paragraph about the student and his or her family. Answer these questions in your paragraph:

   Where is the student from?
   Where does the student live now?
   How many siblings does the student have?

4. Make a family tree for the student.

5. Make a one-day planner for the student.
   Student 1: Maybe he has to work 8 hours.
   Student 2: I think he should have three children he has to take to school.
   Student 3: How about going to the gym?
   Student 4: What about dinner?

   Write down all the ideas and then choose which ones you want to include.

6. Make a one-month calendar for the student.

7. Report to the class.

COLLABORATION:
Sharing Ideas and Brainstorming
Write everything that you can think of for the question, good or not so good. Sometimes ideas that you don't like help your team think of other ideas.

Reading Challenge

A Match the words and definitions.

_____ 1. Life expectancy   a. not enough or not a sufficient amount of something

_____ 2. Shrinking   b. how long do we think people will live

_____ 3. Shortage   c. getting smaller

B Tell a group about your family. Answer the questions.

1. Is your family big or small?   2. How many people are in an average family in your country?

C Read the article. Use a dictionary to look up any new words.

D Choose the correct answers.

1. What is happening to the world's life expectancy?
   a. It's going up.   b. It's staying the same.   c. It's going down.

2. What was the world fertility rate in 1950?
   a. three   b. five   c. seven

3. What was the world fertility rate in 2021?
   a. under two   b. over two   c. almost seven

E **INFER** Read the sentences from the text and answer the questions. Use the context.

1. In line 1, what does *fertility rate* mean?
   a. *Fertility rate* means the average number of children born.
   b. *Fertility rate* means all children born in the world.
   c. *Fertility rate* means the number of children who die at a young age.

2. In line 8, what does *workforce* mean?
   a. *Workforce* means machines working.
   b. *Workforce* means workers in jobs.
   c. *Workforce* means people who retire early.

3. In line 9, what does *researchers* mean?
   a. *Researchers* are people who look for information and study things.
   b. *Researchers* are people who worry about things.
   c. *Researchers* are mothers who care about their children.

4. In line 13, what does *resist* mean?
   a. *Resist* means to like something.
   b. *Resist* means to use something.
   c. *Resist* means to try not to do something.

F Work in a group. In your notebook, make a list of some examples of automation over the last 20 years.

A Shrinking Population

Family size around the world is shrinking. In 1950, the world **fertility rate** was five children for every woman. In 2021, it was under two children for every woman. In Mexico, it was almost seven in 1950, and in 2021, it was just over two. Do lowering fertility rates cause problems in the world?

Nowadays, people are living longer. If the fertility rate falls below two children for every woman, there will be fewer young people in the world. In 1950, world life expectancy was 46 years. In 2021, it was over 72 years! In the United States the current life expectancy is greater than 72 years. Many people stop working at 65, so what will happen to the **workforce**? Some **researchers** are worried that in 20 years, fewer workers will be supporting more people who don't work. Will there be enough workers to keep society moving?

Of course, one solution for a worker shortage would be to have more children. Another might be machines that can do the work of many workers. This is called automation. Some people **resist** automation because they don't want to lose their jobs to machines. What do you think is the solution?

Mechanics use a device to find problems in a car.

2 Let's Go Shopping!

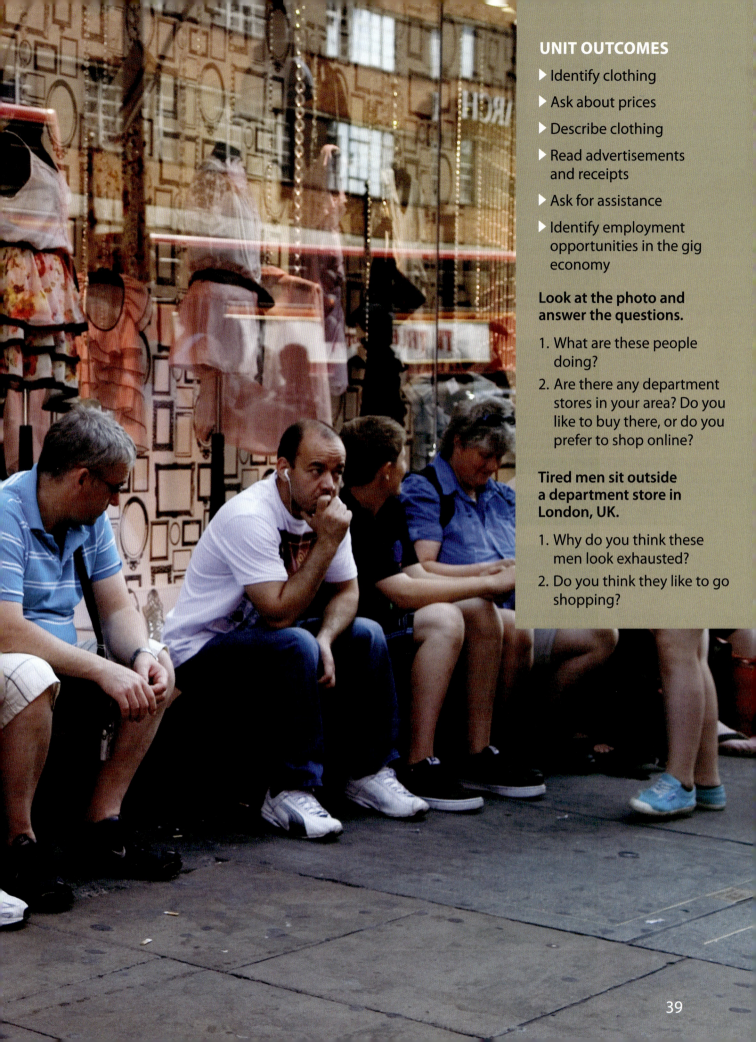

UNIT OUTCOMES

▶ Identify clothing
▶ Ask about prices
▶ Describe clothing
▶ Read advertisements and receipts
▶ Ask for assistance
▶ Identify employment opportunities in the gig economy

Look at the photo and answer the questions.

1. What are these people doing?
2. Are there any department stores in your area? Do you like to buy there, or do you prefer to shop online?

Tired men sit outside a department store in London, UK.

1. Why do you think these men look exhausted?
2. Do you think they like to go shopping?

LESSON 1

What We Wear

GOAL ▶ Identify clothing

A PREDICT Look at the pictures. Answer the questions in full sentences.

1. Where in the United States do you think the family is in Picture A?

   I think the family is in _____.

2. What do you think is the temperature in Picture A?

   I think the temperature is _____.

3. Where in the United States do you think the family is in Picture B?

   _____.

4. What do you think is the temperature in Picture B?

   _____.

B Listen and check your answers in A. 🎧

C CLASSIFY Listen again and complete the chart. 🎧

Clothes for Hot Weather	Clothes for Cool Weather	Clothes for Cold Weather

40 UNIT 2

D Look at the picture. What clothes can you see?

E Write the letters from the picture next to each word.

_____ blouse   _____ jeans   _____ shoes   _____ sneakers   _____ t-shirts

_____ dress   _____ shirts   _____ shorts   _____ suit   _____ ties

F **CLASSIFY** Work in a group. Sort the clothes in E.

Formal	Informal

LESSON 1

G Study the charts with your classmates and teacher.

Simple Present		
Subject	Verb	
I / You / We / They	wear	sweaters. t-shirts. shoes.
He / She	wears*	
Pronunciation: */z/		

Negative Simple Present			
Subject	Negative	Base Verb	
I / You / We / They	don't	wear	pants. hats. sandals.
He / She	doesn't		

H **IDENTIFY** Write sentences about the people in the photos.

1. What does he wear to work?

   He wears a suit to work.

   _____

   _____

2. What does she wear to meet friends?

   She wears jeans.

   _____

   _____

I Talk in a group about what the people in **H** wear to work and to meet friends.

EXAMPLE: He wears a suit to work. She wears jeans to meet friends.

J Write sentences about what you and your classmates wear to school.

1. My classmate wears _____ to school. _____ (pronoun) doesn't wear _____.

2. I wear _____ to school. I don't wear _____.

3. My classmates _____ to school. They don't _____.

LESSON 2

How Much Is It?
GOAL ▶ Ask about prices

A Look at Aaliyah and Ikel. Write the words next to the clothes.

| baseball cap | coat | sandals | shorts | sweater |
| boots | gloves | scarf | sunglasses | t-shirt |

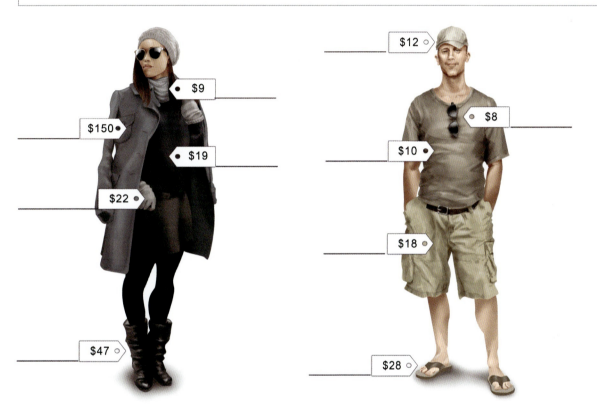

B Practice the conversation. Use the information in A to make new conversations.

Student A: How much is Aaliyah's <u>scarf</u>?

Student B: It's <u>$9.00</u>.

Student B: How much are the <u>sunglasses</u>?

Student A: They're <u>$8.00</u>.

C CALCULATE What is the total cost of the clothing?

1. How much are Aaliyah's clothes? _____

2. How much are Ikel's clothes? _____

LESSON 2   43

D Study the chart with your classmates and teacher.

Comparative and Superlative Adjectives		
Adjective	**Comparative Adjective**	**Superlative Adjective**
cheap	cheaper	the cheapest
expensive	more expensive	the most expensive

E COMPARE Work with a partner. Ask about the prices of clothes in A. Write them.

Ask your partner about Aaliyah's clothes.

Student A: How much is the coat?

Student B: It's $150.00.

the cheapest — coat ($150) — the most expensive

Ask your partner about Ikel's clothes.

Student B: How much are the sunglasses?

Student A: They're $8.00.

sunglasses ($8) — the cheapest — the most expensive

F ORGANIZE Listen to the conversations. Then put the clothing in order from the cheapest to the most expensive.

	Clothing	Price
the cheapest ↓ the most expensive		

44 UNIT 2

G INTERPRET Answer questions about the receipts.

RECEIPT	RECEIPT	RECEIPT
Dress $88.89	Suit $299.99	Shoes $34.99
8% Sales Tax $7.11	6.25% Sales Tax $18.74	5.75% Sales Tax $2.01
TOTAL $96.00	TOTAL $318.73	TOTAL $37.00
Customer Copy	Customer Copy	Customer Copy

1. How much is the dress? _____
2. How much is the tax on the suit? _____
3. How much is the total for the shoes? _____

H Practice the conversation. Use the receipts in **G** to make new conversations.

Customer: Excuse me. How much is the dress?

Salesperson: It's $88.89.

Customer: How much is it with tax?

Salesperson: It's $96.00 with tax.

Customer: Great! / No, thanks. That's too expensive.

I APPLY What clothing do you need? You have $300. Look at some online stores, make a list, and share it with the class.

SALES TAX Most of the time, prices for goods don't include the sales tax. This amount is not the same in every city or state. When making online purchases, the amount of sales tax you pay is calculated after you enter your delivery address.

Remember to keep your receipt. You might need it to return your items.

LESSON 2 45

LESSON 3

What Are They Wearing?

GOAL ▶ Describe clothing

A Look at the sizes, colors, patterns, and styles of the clothes in the picture. Look up any new words in a dictionary.

Size: extra large
Color: red and white
Pattern: striped
Style: long-sleeved

Size: large
Color: pink and yellow
Pattern: flowered
Style: short-sleeved

Size: small
Color: blue and green
Style: long-sleeved

Size: medium
Color: orange
Style: short-sleeved

B **IDENTIFY** Listen and write the names of the Nguyen brothers. 🎧

So   Duong   Tan   Diem

1. _____
2. _____
3. _____
4. _____
5. _____
6. _____

46   UNIT 2

C Study the chart with your classmates and teacher.

Present Continuous			
Subject	Be	Verb + -ing	Example Sentence
I	am	wearing	I **am wearing** a sweater right now.
You / We / They	are		We **are wearing** shoes.
He / She / It	is		She **is wearing** sunglasses today.

D Complete the sentences with the present continuous form of *wear*.

1. He _____ a flowered shirt.

2. The woman _____ a beautiful dress.

3. They _____ new clothes.

4. Alan and I _____ sunglasses.

5. You _____ a flowered blouse.

6. I _____ a striped shirt.

E Write two sentences about each Nguyen brother from B.

1. *So is wearing a blue shirt and black pants. He is not wearing glasses.*

2. _____

3. _____

4. _____

LESSON 3   47

F Look at the ad. Describe what the people are wearing.

G Work with a partner. Practice the conversation. Use the ad in F to make new conversations.

Student A: What is this man wearing in this picture? (points to picture)

Student B: He is wearing a black suit and a red tie.

H **APPLY** Write sentences about what you and your partner are wearing.

1. I _____.
2. I _____.
3. I _____.
4. I _____.
5. My partner _____.
6. My partner _____.
7. My partner _____.
8. My partner _____.

LESSON 4 Advertisements

GOAL ▶ Read advertisements and receipts

A PREDICT Read the ad and guess the sale prices. Then listen and fill in the missing information.

B Listen again and check (✓) the clothing that needs a coupon.

_____ 1. men's shirts   _____ 2. women's pants   _____ 3. sneakers   _____ 4. baseball caps

C Practice the conversation with a partner. Then use the ad in **A** to make new conversations.

Salesperson: Can I help you?

Customer: How much are the shirts?

Salesperson: The shirts are $26.00.

Customer: The ad says they are $4.00 off.

Salesperson: Sorry. You're right. They are $22.00.

Off
Read how *off* is used to talk about savings.
The shirts are $4.00 off.
They are $4.00 off with a coupon.
They are $4.00 off the regular price.

D INTERPRET Read the receipt and choose the correct answers. Then use the ad in **A** to complete the receipt. Use the sale price of each item.

Sam's Uniform Company
20 Row St., Chicago IL, 60601

01/19/23   3:05 PM
Store 126   Register 003
Salesperson: 57968

Item	Qty.	Price	Amount
034521 Men's shirt	3		$
CZ0197 Women's pants	2		$
CZ0197 Men's boots	1	37.00	$
CZ0197 Women's belts	2	18.00	$
		Subtotal	$
		Total Tax	$13.18
		Total USD	$

1. How many shirts are on the receipt?
   _____

2. What does *price* mean?
   a. how many
   b. how much for one
   c. total price

3. What does *item* mean?
   a. the price
   b. how many
   c. kind of clothing

4. What does *subtotal* mean?
   a. price for all items
   b. coupon price
   c. number of items

E CALCULATE Complete the receipt.

Addy's Clothing Company
25 First St., Chicago IL, 60601

04/08/23   10:43 AM
Store 50607   Register 2
Salesperson: 3662582

Item	Qty.	Price	Amount
0-ZD68 Men's shirt	2	32.00	$
33-1025 Women's pants	4	34.00	$
D-M310 Men's boots	1	48.00	$
A-118706 Women's belts	2	16.00	$
		Subtotal	$280.00
		Total Tax	$16.00
		Total USD	$

F Read. Why does this person shop at Addy's Clothing Company?

> I shop at Addy's because it's close to my house on First Street. Addy's has good prices. The prices at Sam's are also good, but it's far away. I think they have boots on sale for $37. Addy's boots are more expensive, but I don't need boots right now. Maybe they will be on sale in the future.

G **COMPARE** Look at the receipts in D and E. Complete the graph about Sam's Uniform Company and Addy's Clothing Company.

H Read the information for an online store. Then answer the questions.

Life ONLINE

1. How can you get ten percent off your purchase on this website?

   a. by clicking on the "X"

   b. by entering your phone number

   c. by entering your email address

2. How can you cancel the messages?

   a. by replying "STOP"

   b. by replying "HELP"

   c. by entering your mobile number

LESSON 5

Which one Do You Want?

GOAL ▶ Ask for assistance

A Look at the photo. Where is the customer? Who is the customer speaking to?

B Listen to the conversation between a customer and a salesperson.

Customer:	Excuse me. Can you help me?
Salesperson:	Sure. What can I do for you?
Customer:	I want a <u>cap</u> and a few other things.
Salesperson:	What color do you want?
Customer:	I want this <u>black</u> one, but it is too expensive.
Salesperson:	Oh, I'm sorry. Maybe a <u>yellow</u> one?
Customer:	I prefer <u>orange</u>.

C **DISTINGUISH** Listen to the conversations. Choose the items the customer wants.

1. orange cap	red cap	blue cap	yellow cap
2. black umbrella	blue umbrella	green umbrella	red umbrella
3. gray jeans	brown jeans	blue jeans	black jeans
4. brown socks	white socks	black socks	yellow socks

D Make a conversation between a customer and a salesperson using the information in C.

A saleswoman helps a customer shop for clothes.

E Study the chart with your classmates and teacher.

	Near	Not Near
Singular	this	that
Plural	these	those

F Look at the picture. Complete the sentences with *this, that, these,* or *those.*

1. _____ cap is yellow and _____ cap is orange.

2. _____ umbrella is red and _____ umbrella is green.

3. _____ jeans are blue and _____ jeans are black.

4. _____ socks are white and _____ socks are yellow.

G Practice the conversation. Use *this, that, these,* or *those* to make new conversations.

Student A: What color is *that* shirt?

Student B: It's purple.

Student B: What color are *these* pants?

Student A: They're black.

LESSON 5 53

H Look at the reasons for returning clothing. Have you ever returned something? What was your reason?

> I don't like the color.
> It's damaged.
> It doesn't fit.
> I don't like it.
> It's the wrong size.

I Read and listen to the conversation.

Manager:	May I help you?
Customer:	Yes, I want to return these jeans.
Manager:	Yes, sir. Why do you want to return them?
Customer:	They don't fit.
Manager:	OK. Do you have the receipt?
Customer:	Oh, no, I don't.
Manager:	I'm sorry, you can't return them without a receipt, but you can exchange them.
Customer:	OK. Maybe I will get those brown ones over there.
Manager:	That's fine, sir.

J Work with a partner. Make new conversations using the items and reasons.

Manager: May I help you?
Customer: Yes, I want to return _____.
Manager: Of course. Why do you want to return _____?
Customer: _____

> blouse / damaged
> shoes / don't fit
> shorts / don't like
> dress / wrong size

Singular and plural

Singular	Plural
return it	return them
exchange it	exchange them

K **CREATE** Imagine that you need to return something. Write a new conversation with a partner and perform it for the class.

LESSON 6: Explore the Workforce

GOAL ▶ Identify employment opportunities in the gig economy

A Read about gig workers. With the class, make a list of different gig work opportunities.

> Gig workers are people who do temporary service work like driving people, delivering groceries, or walking dogs. Gig workers may have other workforce skills, but the flexibility allows these workers to decide when they want or need to work.

Vocabulary Review: Synonyms
Words that mean the same thing or almost the same thing.

Examples:

big	large
talk	speak
advantage	pro

B **INTERPRET** Study the infographic. Use a dictionary to find synonyms.

1. What is a synonym for *advantages*?

   _____

2. What is a synonym for *disadvantages*?

   _____

3. Use a dictionary and find a synonym for *commute*.

   _____

4. Use a dictionary and find a synonym for *casual*.

   _____

GIG WORKERS
WHAT ARE THE ADVANTAGES AND DISADVANTAGES?

PROS

Freedom
Be your own boss.

Flexibility
Decide when and where you work.

Choice
Choose who you want to work with.

Avoid the commute
Work from home if you want.

Be casual
no need for formal clothing

CONS

No fixed income
no work, no pay

Career growth
not many opportunities to grow

Isolation
no coworkers

Hustling
always looking for new jobs

No benefits or paid time off

No parental leave

Juggling all your clients

C Study the cons in the chart. Use a dictionary and write short definitions.

1. hustling: _____
2. isolation: _____
3. juggling: _____
4. parental leave: _____

D **INTERPRET** Study the requirements for a gig driving service. Which requirements do you meet now?

E In a group, write synonyms from the chart for the terms.

1. Authorized to drive: _____

2. Communication device: _____

3. History with the law: _____

4. Qualified Automobile: _____

F **INVESTIGATE** In a group, research online how much money you can make a year doing a driving gig service.

G In a group, discuss if you would enjoy or not enjoy a job driving people. Why?

GIG DRIVER REQUIREMENTS

Own a Smartphone
Drivers must have smartphones. Jobs for rides are accepted and managed by smartphones.

Age
All drivers must be 21 years or older.

Be a Licensed Driver
All drivers must have a driver's license and one year's experience driving.

Have the Documents
All drivers who are not citizens must have documentation that shows they can work in the United States.

Have an Eligible Car
Drivers' cars must be in good condition, clean, and safe. Cars should not be more than 15 years old.

Background Check
Drivers must have no felony convictions.

Driving History Check
Drivers must not have too many accidents or major driving infractions.

H **SELF-EVALUATE** Check what is true about you.

☐ I need extra money for home expenses.

☐ I need a job, but I need more time with my family.

☐ I want control of my schedule.

☐ I need to make money right now.

☐ I need to make money while looking for a better job or going to school.

I **INVESTIGATE** In a group, follow the steps and research gig careers.

1. Go to your favorite search engine.

2. Type "gig careers."

3. Open at least three webpages.

4. On a separate piece of paper, write five new things you learn.

J Some people walk dogs as a side job. Leslie Campbell, from California, started a business walking dogs more than 15 years ago. Do you prefer to spend your days inside an office, or do you like to work outside? Do you like animals? What do you think about walking of dogs as a job? Talk to a partner.

Leslie Campbell celebrated National Dog Day by posting this photo by photographer Johanna Siegmann. Here she is in her car with "the amazing dogs" in her life.

Review

A Look at the ads from a clothing store. Underline any important information.

1. SALE PRICE $14 — REGULAR PRICE $28 — SIZE M AND L ONLY
2. COUPON REQUIRED — SALE PRICE $45 — REGULAR PRICE $52 — SMALL SIZES ONLY
3. ALL SIZES — SALE PRICE $24 — SAVINGS $5 — NO COUPON NECESSARY

4. ALL SIZES AND COLORS — SALE PRICE $15 WITH COUPON — REGULAR PRICE $25
5. NO COUPON REQUIRED — SALE PRICE $22 — REGULAR PRICE $25 — ALL SIZES
6. ALL SIZES AND COLORS — SALE PRICE $34 WITH COUPON — REGULAR PRICE $44

B Complete the information using the ads in **A**.

1. Item: _____
   Need Coupon? _____
   Color: _____
   Style: _____
   Size: _____
   Sale Price: $ _____
   Regular Price: $ ____
   Savings: $ _____

2. Item: _____
   Need Coupon? _____
   Color: _____
   Size: _____
   Sale Price: $ _____
   Regular Price: $ ____
   Savings: $ _____

3. Item: _____
   Need Coupon? _____
   Color: _____
   Size: _____
   Sale Price: $ _____
   Regular Price: $ ____
   Savings: $ _____

4. Item: _____
   Need Coupon? _____
   Color: _____
   Style: _____
   Size: _____
   Sale Price: $ _____
   Regular Price: $ ____
   Savings: $ _____

5. Item: _____
   Need Coupon? _____
   Color: _____
   Size: _____
   Sale Price: $ _____
   Regular Price: $ ____
   Savings: $ _____

6. Item: _____
   Need Coupon? _____
   Color: _____
   Size: _____
   Sale Price: $ _____
   Regular Price: $ ____
   Savings: $ _____

Learner Log

I can identify clothing. ☐ Yes ☐ No ☐ Maybe

I can describe clothing. ☐ Yes ☐ No ☐ Maybe

C Read the receipts and answer the questions.

Lana's BOUTIQUE	Clothing for Less	THE TRUE Shopper
Women's boots..........$52.55	Women's boots..........$38.55	Women's boots..........$60.00
Women's pants..........$34.50	Women's pants..........$40.00	Women's pants..........$44.00
Belt..........$18.95	Belt..........$12.95	Belt..........$24.50
Blouse..........$42.50	Blouse..........$38.50	Blouse..........$36.95
TOTAL..........$148.50	TOTAL..........$130.00	TOTAL..........$165.45
	Customer Copy	No Refunds without Receipt

1. Which store has the lowest total? _____

2. Where are blouses the cheapest? _____

3. Where are blouses the most expensive? _____

4. Which store has women's pants cheaper than Clothing for Less? _____

5. Which store has blouses more expensive than Clothing for Less? _____

6. Which do you think is the best store? _____

D Complete the sentences with the present continuous form of *wear*.

1. Maria _____is wearing_____ red pants and a pink blouse.

2. Alan _____ new shoes and socks.

3. Marjorie and Paula _____ beautiful dresses.

4. The children _____ shorts.

5. I _____ a suit and tie.

6. We _____ coats.

7. She _____ a new scarf.

Learner Log   I can read ads and receipts.   I can ask about prices.
☐ Yes ☐ No ☐ Maybe   ☐ Yes ☐ No ☐ Maybe

REVIEW 59

Review

E Write three things you can say if you want to make a return.

1. _____
2. _____
3. _____

F Look at the picture. Complete the sentences below with *this, that, these,* or *those*.

1. _____ white shirt is perfect. I don't want _____ blue one.
2. _____ white shoes are great, but I think I want _____ blue ones.
3. _____ shirt is cheap. _____ shirt is better, but it is too expensive.
4. _____ table has white sneakers on it.

G Write what you and your partner are wearing right now.

You: _____
_____
_____

Your partner: _____
_____

Learner Log   I can ask for assistance.
☐ Yes   ☐ No   ☐ Maybe

Team Project

Design a Clothing Store
SOFT SKILL ▶ Collaboration

In this project, you are going to design your own clothing store and create an advertisement for it.

1. Form a team of four or five students. In your team, you need:

Position	Job Description	Student Name
Student 1: **Team Leader**	Check that everyone speaks English. Check that everyone participates.	
Student 2: **Artist**	Design an advertisement with help from the team.	
Student 3: **Sales Specialist**	Write a conversation and practice it with your team.	
Students 4/5: **Spokespeople**	Prepare a class presentation with help from the team.	

2. Choose a name for your store. What do you sell? Women's clothes? Men's clothes? Children's clothes?

   Team Leader: Does anyone have an idea?
   Monica, what do you think?
   Tien, do you agree?
   What are some other ideas?

   COLLABORATION:
   Coordinating with Others
   Before you make a decision, it is important to make sure all group members have an opportunity to participate.

3. Make a list of clothing you sell on a piece of paper. List at least eight items. Describe the clothing by size, color, pattern, and price. Are your clothes for work, sports, or school?

4. Draw or find and cut out pictures of the clothing items in your store. Make an advertisement for your store using the pictures of the items.

5. Practice asking for prices, selling clothing, and returning clothing with your teammates.

6. Present your advertisement to the class.

Reading Challenge

A Look at the photos. What do you notice?

B Make a list of the clothing in each photo.

1.	2.

C **COMPARE** Answer the questions about the photos with a partner.

1. Which photo(s) do you think make the people look more intelligent? Why?
2. Which photo(s) do you think make them look more comfortable? Why?
3. Which photo(s) do you think make them look more prepared for work? Why?
4. Which photo(s) do you think make them look more calm and relaxed? Why?

D **INFER** Read the title of the text. What do you think it is about?

E Read the text.

F What is the main idea of the text?

a. Clothes cannot speak.

b. People make assumptions based on clothing.

c. People who wear glasses are smart.

d. Clothing is a personal choice.

G What does the word *arrogant* mean in line 6?

a. angry

b. friendly

c. self-important

d. comfortable

H Review your ideas in **C**. What assumptions did you make? Why?

62 UNIT 2

1.

2.

What Do Your Clothes Say about You?

Are you more intelligent if you wear glasses? Are you unprofessional if you don't wear a suit to the office? Many people think this is true. We all make *assumptions* about people based on their clothing.

Tony used to work as a bartender. He says that he got bigger tips when he wore
5   glasses. He also says that people thought he was more intelligent when he wore a nice shirt and tie. On the other hand, Tony says his friends think he seems **arrogant** when he wears a suit.

When we don't know a person, we make assumptions based on their appearance. These assumptions can be wrong, but first impressions count, and if we want to show
10   our professional side, we need to think carefully about what we wear. If two people attend a formal job interview, and one wears a suit while the other wears a t-shirt and jeans, what message does that communicate to the interviewer?

Our clothes tell a personal story and communicate messages. What stories will your clothes tell?

---
assumption something people think is true, without proof
bartender someone who makes and serves drinks at a bar or restaurant

READING CHALLENGE

3 Food and Nutrition

UNIT OUTCOMES

▸ Read a menu
▸ Make a shopping list
▸ Locate items in a supermarket
▸ Identify healthy foods
▸ Read recipes
▸ Identify food-related career options

Look at the photo and answer the questions.

1. What kinds of food do they sell in this market?
2. What do you think this man's job is?
3. Do you think this man enjoys his job? Why?
4. This market is in Seattle, Washington. Do you buy food in a place like this?
5. You have $80. What fish do you buy for dinner with your friends?

LESSON 1

Augustin's Restaurant

GOAL ▶ Read a menu

A **PREDICT** Look at Gabriel. Where is he? What is his job?

B Close your book and listen to Gabriel's story. Then open your book and read. 🎧

> My name is Gabriel. I'm a cook in my father's restaurant. His name is Augustin. My mother, sister, and brother work here, too. We have American food in our restaurant. I want to have some food from other countries, too. Maybe someday we can have an international restaurant.

C Choose the correct answers.

1. Gabriel works in a restaurant.	True	False
2. Gabriel only cooks American food in his father's restaurant.	True	False
3. His sister doesn't work in the restaurant.	True	False
4. He wants the restaurant to have food from different countries.	True	False

D INTERPRET Read the menu. What do you want for lunch? Calculate the cost.

Augustin's Restaurant
LUNCH MENU

Soups and Salads
Caesar salad	$4.49
Dinner salad	$10.99
Potato soup	$5.99

Main Courses
(All main courses come with the vegetable of the day.)
Sirloin steak and potatoes	$22.00
Fried chicken and french fries	$14.99

Beverages
Soda	$3.39
Milk	$3.00
Coffee	$2.89
Tea	$3.75

Sandwiches
Big burger	$9.99
Big cheeseburger	$12.99
Super burger combo	$16.49
Turkey sandwich	$11.25

Desserts
Chocolate cake	$6.99
Cheesecake	$7.75
Vanilla or chocolate ice cream	$3.75
Fresh fruit	$4.00

Side Orders
French fries	$3.85
Potato chips	$2.85
Rice	$3.25
Beans	$3.25
Vegetable of the day	$4.00

E CALCULATE Listen to the people ordering food in a restaurant. Write down the orders and calculate the cost.

Table No. 1	Check No. 1001	
1	Super burger combo	$ 16.49
1	Dinner salad	$ 10.99
		$
		$
		$
Total:		$

Table No. 2	Check No. 1002	
		$
		$
		$
		$
		$
Total:		$

Table No. 3	Check No. 1003	
		$
		$
		$
		$
		$
Total:		$

F Study the chart with your classmates and teacher.

Questions with *Can*			
Can	Pronoun	Base Verb	Example Question
Can	I	take help	Can I take your order? Can I help you?
Can	you		Can you take my order? Can you take our order, please? Can you help me? Can you help us?

G Practice the conversation. Use the menu in D to make new conversations.

Server: Can I take your order?

Customer: Yes, I want a Caesar salad, please.

H **CREATE** Work in a group. Make a menu. Include food from your home country.

Soups and Salads	Price	Side Orders	Price
_____	$ ____	_____	$ ____
_____	$ ____	_____	$ ____
Sandwiches	Price	Beverages	Price
_____	$ ____	_____	$ ____
_____	$ ____	_____	$ ____
Main Courses	Price	Desserts	Price
_____	$ ____	_____	$ ____
_____	$ ____	_____	$ ____

LESSON 2

Do We Need Carrots?

GOAL ▶ Make a shopping list

A PREDICT Look at the picture. What are Augustin and Silvia doing?

B Read the paragraph. Who makes the shopping list?

> Augustin is the owner of the family restaurant. Every Thursday morning, he and his wife, Silvia, make a shopping list. In the afternoon, Augustin visits different stores to buy the supplies for the week.

C Listen to Augustin and Silvia make their shopping list. Check (✓) each item they need.

- ☐ bacon
- ☐ fresh fruit
- ☐ sugar
- ☐ carrots
- ☑ ground beef
- ☐ tomatoes
- ☐ chicken
- ☐ ham
- ☐ tuna fish
- ☐ flour
- ☐ lettuce
- ☐ turkey

D Write sentences about what Augustin and Silvia need and don't need.

1. They need ground beef.
2. They don't need turkey, tuna fish, or chicken.
3. _____
4. _____
5. _____

E IDENTIFY Complete Augustin's shopping list with the words from the photos.

carton(s)   box(es)   jar(s)   pound(s)

loaf (loaves)   bottle(s)   can(s)   gallon(s)

Shopping List

- milk 3 __gallons__
- flour 2 __bags__
- tomatoes 5 _____
- bread 3 _____
- cake mix 2 _____
- ice cream 4 _____
- ground beef 2 _____
- sugar 3 __bags__
- jam 1 _____
- oil 2 _____
- oranges 3 _____
- chicken soup 4 _____

Plurals 🎧

/s/	/z/		/ɪz/
carrots	cartons	loaves	boxes
soups	pounds	bags	oranges
cakes	jars	cans	sandwiches
	bottles	gallons	

F Practice the conversation with a partner. Use items from the shopping list to make new conversations.

Augustin: Do we need any <u>milk</u> at the store?

Silvia: Yes, we need some <u>milk</u>.

Augustin: How many <u>gallons</u> do we need?

Silvia: We need <u>three gallons</u>.

Some / Any	
Question	Do we need **any** milk?
Statement	We need **some** milk.

G Study the chart with your classmates and teacher.

Count and Noncount Nouns		
Count Nouns	Use *many* with nouns you can count.	How *many* tomatoes do we need? How *many* pounds of tomatoes do we need?
Noncount Nouns	Use *much* with nouns you cannot count.	How *much* flour do we need? How *much* rice do we need?

H Complete the sentences with *much* or *many*.

1. How _____ bananas do we need?
2. How _____ bottles of oil do we need?
3. How _____ oil do we need?
4. How _____ flour do we need?
5. How _____ apples do we need?
6. How _____ pounds of apples do we need?

I **PLAN** Work in a group. You are planning a party for twenty people. Make a shopping list on a separate piece of paper.

J **APPLY** Go online and find a store to purchase your items. Find the total cost of your food items in I and share with the class.

Some people get creative with their party food. What food items can you see here?

LESSON 2

LESSON 3: At the Supermarket

GOAL ▶ Locate items in a supermarket

A **CLASSIFY** Look at the photos. Discuss the supermarket sections with your teacher and class.

1. Produce

2. Baking

3. Meats

4. Canned Goods

5. Dairy

6. Frozen Foods

B **CLASSIFY** Listen and complete the chart.

Item	Section	Aisle or Location
flour	Baking	Aisle 4
milk		
tomatoes		
chicken		
canned vegetables		
ice cream		

C Work with a partner. Practice the conversation. Make new conversations with *milk, tomatoes, canned corn, chicken, pears, ice cream, butter, soup, sugar,* and *oranges*.

Customer: Excuse me. Where is the flour?

Team Member: It's in Aisle 4.

Customer: Where are the oranges?

Team Member: They are on the right side of the store.

The Verb *Be*	
Singular	Where **is** the flour? It **is** in Aisle 4.
Plural	Where **are** the oranges? They **are** on the right side of the store.

D **INTERPRET** Read the store directory.

Product	Section	Aisle	Product	Section	Aisle	Product	Section	Aisle
Apples	Produce	1	Cheese	Dairy	12	Ice cream	Frozen Foods/Dessert	5
Bread	Bakery	2	Chicken	Meats	back	Lettuce	Produce	1
Brown sugar	Baking	4	Cookies	Bakery	2	Milk	Dairy	12
Butter	Dairy	12	Cream	Dairy	12	Oranges	Produce	1
Cake	Bakery	2	Cucumbers	Produce	1	Pears	Produce	1
Cake mix	Baking	4	Eggs	Dairy	12	Soup	Canned Goods	3
Canned corn	Canned Goods	3	Flour	Baking	4	Sugar	Baking	4
Canned peas	Canned Goods	3	Ground beef	Meats	back	Turkey	Meats	back
Cantaloupe	Produce	1	Ham	Meats	back	Yogurt	Dairy	12

E Answer the questions with complete sentences.

1. Where are the cookies? _They are in the Bakery section in Aisle 2._

2. Where is the brown sugar? _____

3. Where is the ground beef? _____

4. Where are the eggs? _____

F Practice the conversation with a partner. Use the directory in **D** to make new conversations.

Customer: Can you help me? I'm looking for the canned corn.

Store Clerk: It's in the Canned Goods section.

Customer: Where's the Canned Goods section?

Store Clerk: It's in Aisle 3.

Customer: Thanks!

Rhythm

_____ . . _____ .
Where are the cookies?

G PREDICT Read the shopping list. Predict the section for each item. Then listen to the conversation and complete the table.

Shopping list	Section	Aisle or Location
beets		
muffins		
strawberries		
chicken breasts		

H BRAINSTORM In a group, create a cluster diagram on a separate piece of paper with items from your local supermarket.

I Read about buying groceries online.

Buying groceries online is convenient, but it's important to check your order so there are no surprises. Always check the size of containers. Photos online can be misleading. Also, make sure the quantities are correct. And look out for additional fees.

J It's Wednesday, and Nico needs a few groceries before he can go to the store on Saturday. Work with a partner. Look at Nico's online order and identify any problems.

GROCERY STORE | ONLINE ORDER

Item	Item Price	Quantity	Price
water 12 pack (12 x 12.5 fl oz)	$3.49	12	$41.88
apples $3.29 / lb	$3.29	15	$49.35
strawberries (2 lb container)	$4.99	1	$4.99
milk (quart)	$1.75	1	$1.75
peach yogurt (32 oz)	$2.30	1	$2.30
chocolate ice cream (48 oz)	$7.50	2	$15.00
		Delivery Fee	$20.00
		(free delivery on orders over $120.00 only)	
		Total	**$135.27**

LESSON 4
A Healthy Diet
GOAL ▶ Identify healthy foods

A Close your books and listen. Then read about nutrition and discuss the paragraph with the class.

> Nutrition means the food we eat and how much we eat of each food group. Good nutrition is important. When we eat good food, our bodies are stronger, and we stay healthy. MyPlate is a guide that helps people choose the best foods for a balanced diet. It's healthy to eat food from each of the main food groups.

B **INTERPRET** Look at the MyPlate nutrition guide. What foods can you put into the different groups?

C **CLASSIFY** Write nutritious foods for each category.

Grains	Vegetables	Fruits	Protein	Dairy

D Augustin and his family didn't eat together yesterday because they were very busy. Read what everyone ate.

Silvia

Breakfast: cereal and milk
Lunch: green salad and fruit juice
Dinner: spaghetti with meatballs, and ice cream

Augustin

Breakfast: coffee
Lunch: sausage, beans, rice, and water
Dinner: cheese, bread, green salad, and fruit

Fernando

Breakfast: fruit, cereal, milk, and toast
Lunch: pepperoni pizza and milk
Dinner: fried chicken and a baked potato

Rosa

Breakfast: toast and coffee
Lunch: soup, bread, fruit, and yogurt
Dinner: turkey, potatoes, green salad, and water

Gabriel

Breakfast: doughnut and coffee
Lunch: hamburger, fries, and soda
Dinner: pepperoni pizza and beer

Simple Past: *had / ate*

I **had / ate** . . .
You **had / ate** . . .
He / She **had / ate** . . .

E **RANK** Who has the best diet? In a group, rank the family members in order from the best diet to the worst. *1* is the best.

_____ Silvia

_____ Augustin

_____ Fernando

_____ Rosa

_____ Gabriel

76   UNIT 3

F COMPARE Complete the diagram. Write the foods Rosa and Augustin eat for breakfast, lunch, and dinner.

Rosa
toast
_____
_____
_____
_____

Both
coffee
_____
_____
_____

Augustin
sausage
_____
_____
_____

G APPLY What do you and your family eat for breakfast, lunch, and dinner? Complete the table.

Breakfast	Lunch	Dinner

H Work with a partner. Ask and answer the questions.

1. What do you eat for breakfast? _____

2. What do you eat for lunch? _____

3. What do you eat for dinner? _____

LESSON 4

LESSON 5

Following Instructions

GOAL ▶ Read recipes

A INTERPRET Read the recipe.

Spaghetti and Meatballs

Ingredients: *Serves 6 people*

2 jars of tomato sauce
2 eggs
1 onion
2 packages of spaghetti
2 pounds of ground beef, salt, pepper

Instructions:

1. Cook the pasta according to package directions.
2. Combine the eggs, chopped onion, salt, and pepper in a large bowl. Add the beef and mix well.
3. Shape the mixture into approximately 48 balls and fry until cooked.
4. Heat the tomato sauce for 10 minutes on medium heat.
5. Add the meatballs and simmer for 15 minutes. Then add to pasta and serve.

B Practice the conversation. Use the recipe in **A** to make new conversations.

Student A: How much tomato sauce do we need?
Student B: We need two jars.
Student A: How many?
Student B: Two jars.

How much? / How many?
How many eggs do we need?
How much sauce do we need?

78 UNIT 3

C Read the recipe for mashed potatoes. Underline the new words.

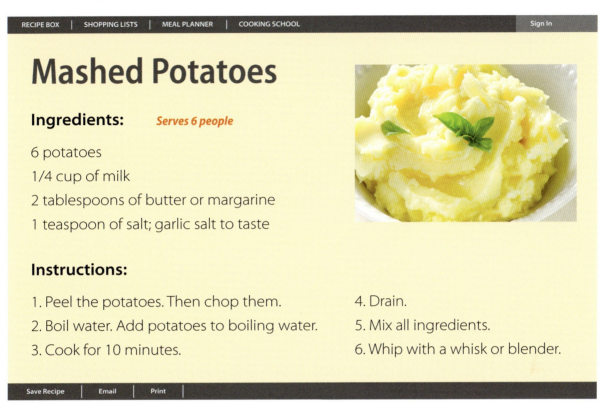

D **SEQUENCE** Match the pictures with the words. Then order the steps.

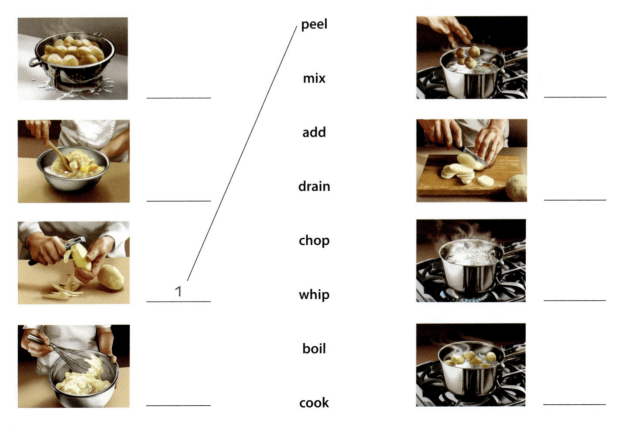

E Study the charts with your classmates and teacher.

Imperatives		
	Base Verb	**Example Sentence**
~~you~~	drain	**Drain** the water.
	chop	**Chop** the potatoes.
	peel	**Peel** the potatoes.

Negative Imperatives			
	Negative	**Base Verb**	**Example Sentence**
~~you~~	do not don't	boil	**Do not boil** the water. (**Don't boil** the water.)
		use	**Do not use** salt. (**Don't use** salt.)
		cook	**Do not cook** in the microwave. (**Don't cook** in the microwave.)

F **SEQUENCE** Listen to the instructions. Number them in the correct order.

1. **Recipe: Cake**

    _____ Bake for 35 minutes.

    _____ Combine cake mix, water, oil, and eggs in a large bowl.

    __1__ Heat oven to 350 degrees.

    _____ Pour mixture into a pan.

2. **Recipe: Tacos**

    _____ Add ground beef, cheese, tomatoes, and lettuce to the fried tortillas.

    _____ Cut tomatoes, onions, cheese, and lettuce.

    _____ Drain grease.

    _____ Fry corn tortillas.

    _____ Fry ground beef.

G **CREATE** In a group, choose a dish and write a recipe on a separate piece of paper.

LESSON 6
Explore the Workforce
GOAL ▶ Identify food-related career options

A INTERPRET Look at the infographic and answer the questions.

1. Which career has the greatest earning potential?
2. Which career has the smallest earning potential?
3. Which career has the greatest openings potential?
4. Which career has the smallest openings potential?

Adjective	Superlative
great (big)	the greatest
	the next greatest
small	the smallest

B ANALYZE Ask your partner questions about the information in **A** and complete the chart with the four careers that have the greatest earning potential in order.

Student A: Which career has the greatest earning potential? How much is it?

Student B: Food scientist, and it's $124,660 a year.

Student A: That's $124,660, right?

Student B: That's right.

Job Title	Potential Salary	Potential Openings
Food scientist		

LESSON 6   81

C Read the text and the information in the chart. Look up new words in a dictionary.

> Chefs are trained cooks. They usually go to school and earn certificates to qualify for jobs in high-end restaurants. Cooking students who want to be chefs have different choices for education. Some want to be master chefs and create a personal way of cooking. Others want to learn just enough to have a steady career. A few may want to go from being a chef to owning a restaurant. Good education choices will help them reach their goals.

	Associate Degree	Bachelor's Degree	Online Certificate
I love cooking. I just don't have a lot of time. I want to cook better. Maybe I will get a part-time job or do catering.			✓
I am interested in the restaurant business. Maybe one day I can own a restaurant.		✓	
I want to become a trained cook as soon as possible. I want to go to school, but I only want to take classes related to cooking.	✓		

D **CLASSIFY** Look at the chart in C. Read the sentences and choose the correct answers.

1. I want to be a chef who gives direction to my assistants in a high-end restaurant.

    ☐ Associate   ☐ Bachelor's   ☐ Online

2. I may want to cook part-time to earn some extra money.

    ☐ Associate   ☐ Bachelor's   ☐ Online

3. I want to know everything about cooking and will study as much as I can to learn about it.

    ☐ Associate   ☐ Bachelor's   ☐ Online

4. I plan to own my own restaurant one day.

    ☐ Associate   ☐ Bachelor's   ☐ Online

5. I want to impress my friends with my cooking skills.

    ☐ Associate   ☐ Bachelor's   ☐ Online

E Work in a group. Discuss which level of education would be best for you in your food-related career. Explain why.

   EXAMPLE: I think the associate level is the best for me because I can make a good salary, but I don't have to go to school for very long.

F SELF-EVALUATE Read the list of characteristics for people who choose a career as a chef. Check what is true about you.

☐ I like to lead people. ☐ I think my ideas are the best ideas.
☐ I am very organized. ☐ I am dependable and responsible.
☐ I work hard. ☐ I like making lists.
☐ I'm a perfectionist. ☐ I like to plan.

G INVESTIGATE Work in a group. Follow the steps and research food-related careers.

1. Go to your favorite search engine.
2. Type "food-related careers."
3. Open at least three webpages.
4. Write five new things you learn.

1. _____
2. _____
3. _____
4. _____
5. _____

H Choose a job title related to food. Go to a job search site online and see if there are any openings within 25 miles of your school or home.

A chef prepares food for customers in the kitchen of a burger bar.

Review

A Read the menu. Fill in the name of each section.

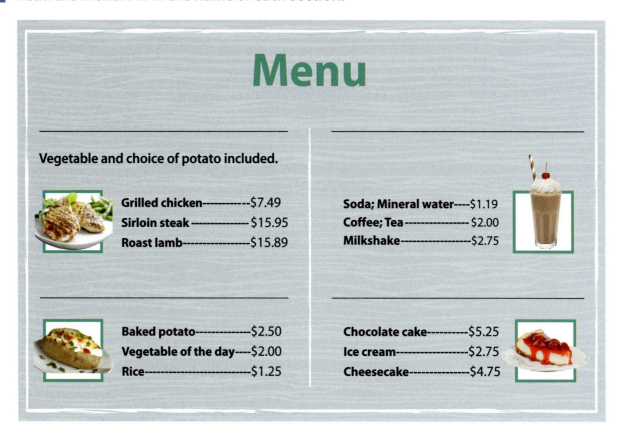

B Number the conversation in the correct order.

_____ **Server:** What do you want to drink?

_____ **Customer:** That's all, thank you.

_____ **Customer:** Yes, I'll have the steak and a baked potato, please.

_____ **Customer:** Mineral water, please.

_____ **Server:** Can I take your order?

_____ **Server:** Anything else?

C Make more conversations with food from the menu in **A**.

Learner Log   I can read a menu. ☐ Yes ☐ No ☐ Maybe   I can make a shopping list. ☐ Yes ☐ No ☐ Maybe

D Write *How much* or *How many*.

1. _____ oranges do we need?
2. _____ tomatoes do we need?
3. _____ milk do we need?
4. _____ gallons of milk do we need?
5. _____ bread do we need?
6. _____ ice cream do we need?

E Write a word from the box under each photo.

| bottle | box | can | carton | gallon | jar | loaf | pound |

1.
_____

2.
_____

3.
_____

4.
_____

5.
_____

6.
_____

7.
_____

8.
_____

Learner Log I can locate items in a supermarket.   I can identify healthy foods.
☐ Yes ☐ No ☐ Maybe   ☐ Yes ☐ No ☐ Maybe

REVIEW 85

Review

F Read the recipe. Underline the verbs in the instructions.

Beef Stew

Ingredients: *Serves 10 people*

- 3 pounds of beef
- 4 carrots
- 1-1/2 onions
- 2 potatoes
- 1 cup of chili sauce
- 1 cup of brown sugar

Instructions:
1. <u>Chop</u> carrots, potatoes, and onions.
2. <u>Boil</u> water. <u>Add</u> potatoes, carrots, and onions to water. <u>Boil</u> for 15 minutes.
3. <u>Cook</u> beef until brown in separate pan.
4. <u>Add</u> chili sauce. <u>Mix</u> in brown sugar.
5. <u>Add</u> all ingredients to vegetables and <u>cook</u> over low heat for two hours.

G Answer the questions about the recipe.

1. What is the recipe for? _____
2. How many people does the recipe serve? _____
3. Write three important ingredients. _____

H Write the section in the supermarket and the food group for each food below.

Food	Section	Food Group
canned green beans	Canned Goods	vegetables
loaf of bread		
onions		
ground beef		
milk		
eggs		

Learner Log I can read recipes.
☐ Yes ☐ No ☐ Maybe

Team Project

Plan a Menu
SOFT SKILL ▶ Active Listening

In this project, you will plan a family menu. You are a family of four or five people. You have $300 to spend on food for the next week. What can you make for breakfast, lunch, and dinner? Make a menu and go shopping.

1. Form a team of four or five students. In your team, you need:

Position	Job Description	Student Name
Student 1: **Team Leader**	Check that everyone speaks English. Check that everyone participates.	
Student 2: **Chef**	Plan meals for the family with help from the team.	
Student 3: **Shopper**	Write a shopping list for the family with help from the team.	
Students 4/5: **Spokespeople**	Prepare a class presentation with help from the team.	

2. Choose a name for your family.

3. Fill in a calendar with your meal plans for breakfast, lunch, and dinner for one week.

   Student 1: Let's have eggs for breakfast and sandwiches for lunch.
   Student 2: That's a good idea. _Eggs and sandwiches._ What about a drink?
   Student 3: How about orange juice for breakfast and water for lunch.
   Student 4: So, let me be sure I understand, you all want _eggs and orange juice for breakfast and sandwiches and water for lunch._ Is that right?

4. Make a shopping list. How much of each item do you need? Estimate the prices of the items on your list. Make sure the total is under $300.

5. Write a recipe for one of your meals.

6. Make a family presentation to the class. Tell the class about the meals on your menu. How much money will you spend? How much money will be left? What can you do with the money that will be left over?

ACTIVE LISTENING:
Effective Communication

Listening very carefully and repeating back what you hear improves communication. It shows someone in a conversation you are listening and that you understand.

Reading Challenge

A **SURVEY** Work in a group. Discuss the questions about shopping habits. Share your answers with the class.

1. How do you choose where to buy groceries or food?
2. Do you get all your food at the same store or do you shop at different stores for good deals?
3. How do you choose what food you buy in the supermarket?
4. Do you think some *brands* are better than others? If yes, what are some examples?
5. Do you *avoid* some types of food in your home? Which ones?

brands companies or producers of a product
avoid to stay away from something

B **DEFINE** Use an online dictionary to look up each word and write the English definition. Then look up a translation to complete the table.

Word	Short Definition	Translation
pesticide		
organic (food)		
gluten		
increase		
conventional		

C Read the text. Underline words you don't know. After you read, look up the new words.

D Choose the main idea for the first two paragraphs.

1. **Paragraph 1:** a. choices b. cheap food c. organic is best
2. **Paragraph 2:** a. health food stores b. organic is expensive c. who sells organic

E A topic sentence describes the main idea of a paragraph. Underline the topic sentences for the first two paragraphs.

F In a group, discuss how you choose what produce you buy. Do you choose organic? Do you think it is too expensive?

G Use your ideas from **F** to write a paragraph on a separate piece of paper. Think carefully about your topic sentence.

People shop at Lancaster Central Market, in Lancaster, PA.

Healthy Choices vs. Budgets 🎧

1   Walk into most supermarkets, and you are faced with choices—maybe too many. The average shopper is looking for something cheap that will feed the family. Some shoppers will look for healthy choices for their families. Organic, natural, hormone-free, sugar-free, gluten-free… the choices are endless.

2   For years, only health food stores carried organic produce. Today, *USDA Organic* labels are on many products in our local supermarkets. Farmer's markets are no exception. For example, at Lancaster Central Market in Lancaster, Pennsylvania—the oldest farmer's market in the US—people can buy certified organic produce, eggs, and even flowers!

3   Organic produce is grown without pesticides and is safer for the environment. So, if health food stores carry organic foods, does that mean they are healthier? The short answer is: probably. There are many studies looking at this question. We do know that there are small increases in some nutrients and very few pesticides in organic produce. So, if it is healthier, why not buy it? You probably already know the answer. Studies have shown that organic foods are as much as 47% more expensive!

4   So, it is up to you and your budget to choose organic or conventional. What will you do?

4 Housing

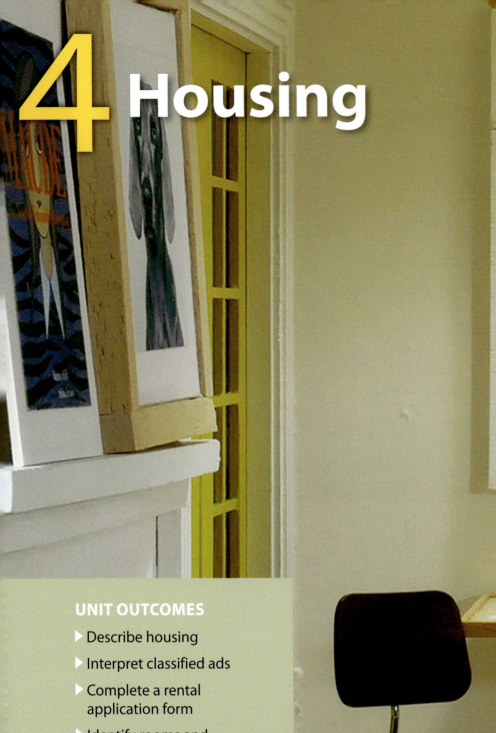

UNIT OUTCOMES

- Describe housing
- Interpret classified ads
- Complete a rental application form
- Identify rooms and furniture
- Make a family budget
- Explore construction-related job opportunities

Look at the photo and answer the questions.

1. What furniture can you see?
2. Which room of a house is the furniture in?

LESSON 1

Looking for a Place to Live
GOAL ▶ Describe housing

A Look at the picture. What are Ernesto and Virginia reading?

B **PREDICT** Work in groups. Why do you think Ernesto and Virginia are looking for a new place to live? Think of three possible reasons.

C Read and listen to the story. Why are Ernesto and his family moving?

> My name is Ernesto. My family and I moved from Venezuela to Fort Myers, Florida, last month. I have a good job here in Fort Myers, but we need to find a place to live. We are living with friends right now in a small house. We need to find a house, apartment, condominium, or mobile home. We need to buy furniture and open a bank account too. We have a lot to do.

D **INTERPRET** Scan the housing advertisements and look at the photos. Write the correct number next to each photo.

1. **FOR RENT**
Three-bedroom house
Rent: $2,500 a month
Address: 315 Madison St.
Contact Agent

2. **MOBILE HOME**
Three-bedroom mobile home
Rent: $950 a month
Address: 1700 Grove St.
Contact Agent

3. **FOR RENT**
Three-bedroom apartment
Rent: $2,000 a month
Address: 200 Atlantic Ave., #211
Contact Agent

4. **CONDO**
Three-bedroom condominium
For sale: $350,000
Address: 12 Shady Glen, #3
Contact Agent

a.  _____

b.  _____

c.  _____

d.  _____

E Study the chart with your classmates and teacher.

Information question	Answer
How **much** is the **house**?	It's $2,500 a month.
What **kind** of **hous**ing is **Num**ber 2?	It's a mobile home.
Where is the condo**min**ium?	It's on Shady Glen.
How many **bed**rooms does the a**part**ment **have**?	It has three bedrooms.

Stress and Rhythm
Emphasize the bold syllables in the chart and say the others quickly.

F Ask a partner information questions about the advertisements in **D**.

LESSON 1 93

G Read about Tamara and Leo. Then ask and answer questions with a partner.

Tamara
I live in a condominium.
It has three bedrooms.
It's on Adams Street.
I like my home.

Leo
I live in an apartment.
It has one bedroom.
It's on Butcher Street.
I don't like my home. I want to move.

H **SURVEY** Do a housing survey in your class. Ask every classmate.

What kind of home do you live in?	Number of classmates
House	
Condominium	
Apartment	
Mobile home	
Other	

I **CREATE** Make a pie chart of your survey. Use the example to help you.

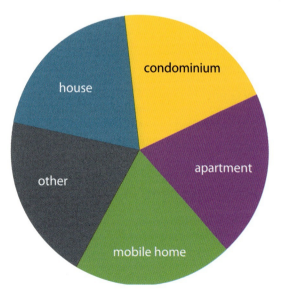
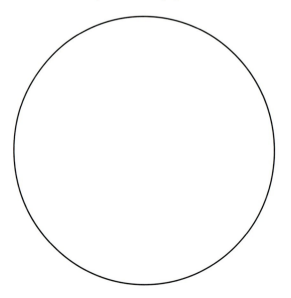

94 UNIT 4

LESSON 2: Finding a Home

GOAL ▶ Interpret classified ads

A SURVEY Talk in groups about your home.

1. What kind of home do you live in?
2. Is your home large or small?
3. How many bedrooms does it have?
4. Is it near public transportation?
5. Is it in the city? If not, where is it?
6. Is your home old or new?

B Listen to the descriptions and point to the correct house.

a.

b.
Balcony

c.

d.

C Match the pictures with the descriptions below.

_____ 1. This large four-bedroom, three-bathroom house is the perfect rental. The house is older but in very good condition. The neighborhood is quiet and comfortable. There is a beautiful view from the balcony. This two-story house rents for $2,500 a month, and utilities are included.

_____ 2. Come and see this small, one-story dream house. It's in a small and friendly neighborhood. This house rents for $1,800 a month. It has one bedroom, one bathroom, and a large kitchen. You will love it when you see it!

_____ 3. This old and small two-bedroom, one-bathroom house has an interesting history—the same owner for 50 years. Rent it for an amazing $1,500 a month.

_____ 4. If you want to rent a big home and money is not important, rent this very large five-bedroom, three-bathroom house with a swimming pool. $3,000 a month.

D   CLASSIFY Complete the table with information from C. Then ask a partner about the houses.

EXAMPLES: Which house has a pool?
Which house has two bedrooms?

	House #1	House #2	House #3	House #4
Bedrooms				
Bathrooms				
Monthly rent				
Amenities				

E   INTERPRET Scan the classified ads for the houses in B. Which ad is for which house? Write the number of the house.

1. HOUSE FOR RENT _____

Two-bedroom, one-bathroom house with fireplace, air-conditioning, and lots of character. Near schools and shopping center.
Rent: $1,500
Address: 2234 Rolling Hills

Contact Agent

2. HOUSE FOR RENT _____

New one-bedroom, one-bathroom house with a large kitchen and dining room.
Utilities paid.
Rent: $1,800
Address: 2200 W. Alton Ave.

Contact Agent

3. AVAILABLE _____

Large house with five bedrooms, three bathrooms, pool, fireplace, air-conditioning, three-car garage, and a large yard.
Near schools.
Rent: $3,000 a month

Contact Agent

4. FOR RENT _____

Four-bedroom, three-bathroom house with air-conditioning in a quiet community.
Two stories.
Utilities paid.
Rent: $2,500 a month

Contact Agent

Amenities

Amenities are extras a home has to improve value. For example: balcony, large kitchen, large backyard, or swimming pool.

F Look at the ads and take turns asking a partner the questions below.

RENTALS		
1. FOR RENT Two-bedroom, two-bathroom condo. Utilities paid and air-conditioning included. Near parks and schools. Dallas City $1,000 More information	**2. FOR RENT** Four-bedroom, three-bathroom house with pool, fireplace, and balcony. 5253 Bountiful Street, Luxury Heights $1,400 More information	**3. FOR RENT** Clean, three-bedroom apartment with air-conditioning. Mountain view. No pets. $1,200 More information
4. FOR RENT One-bedroom, one-bathroom apartment. New carpets. Sycamore St., Costa Mesa $900 More information	**5. FOR RENT** Three-bedroom, one-bathroom condo with air-conditioning. Water included. Bridgemont $1,400 More information	**6. FOR RENT** Like-new, two-bedroom mobile home. Utilities included. Seawall Estates, Newton $1,100 More information

1. Which home is under $1,000 a month?

2. Which homes have air-conditioning?

3. Which home has a mountain view?

4. Which home has three bathrooms?

G **CREATE** In a group, write a classified ad for a home. Answer these questions in your ad.

1. How much is the rent?

2. How many bedrooms are there?

3. How many bathrooms are there?

4. What amenities are there?

5. Who do you contact?

6. What's the phone number?

H **APPLY** Look online to find classified ads for homes in your area. Find a home for yourself. Report to the class.

LESSON 2

LESSON 3: At the Rental Agency

GOAL ▶ Complete a rental application form

A PREDICT Look at the picture. Where are Ernesto and Virginia? What are they doing?

B CLASSIFY Listen to the conversation. What do Ernesto and Virginia need? What do they want? Complete the table.

Needs	Wants
three-bedroom house	

C Work in a group. Look at the ads and choose the best home for Ernesto and Virginia.

1. FOR RENT
Two-bedroom, two-bathroom house with a big yard.
Utilities paid.
Near schools.

Rent: $2,400 a month
Contact Agent

2. FOR RENT
Three-bedroom, two-bathroom apartment with a big living room, a small yard, and a separate garage. Utilities paid. No deposit.

Rent: $1,850 a month
Contact Agent

3. FOR RENT
Three-bedroom, two-story house with garage.
Air-conditioning.
Near schools and shopping.
Rent: $2,650 a month
Contact Agent

4. FOR RENT
Four-bedroom, three-bathroom, one-story condo with a big yard.
No pets.

Rent: $2,200 a month
Contact Agent

D INTERPRET Discuss the rental application form with your classmates and teacher.

RENTAL APPLICATION FORM

Applicant: Ernesto Rojas   Interviewed by: Paula Wharton
Present Address: 33457 Akron Street, Fort Myers, FL 33901
Phone: (239) 555-5059
Prior Address: 42A Los Budares, Carrizal 1203, Miranda, Venezuela
Social Security Number: 123-45-6789   Email Address: rojasernesto11@maildrive.com
Landlord: Fred Wharton   Prior Landlord: N/A
Employer: Shift Manufacturing   Position: Computer Technician
Personal References: James Baker; Lydia Johnson   Relationship: Boss; Supervisor
Co-Applicant or Spouse: Virginia Rojas
Employer: Rosco Metals   Position: Assembly Worker
Personal Reference: George Pratt   Relationship: Supervisor

E Answer the questions about the application form in D.

1. What's Ernesto's present address?

2. What was his address before he came to Florida?

3. What is the name of the company where he works?

4. What is the name of the company where Virginia works?

5. Who are Ernesto's references?

Information Questions		
What is your name?	**Where** did you live before?	**Who** is your employer?
Where do you live now?	**How** long did you live there?	**What** is your position?

F Interview your partner and complete the application for them.

RENTAL APPLICATION FORM

Applicant: _____ Interviewed by: _____

Present Address: _____

Phone: _____

Prior Address: _____

Social Security Number: _____ Email Address: _____

Landlord: _____ Prior Landlord: _____

Employer: _____ Position: _____

Personal References: _____ Relationship: _____

Co-Applicant or Spouse: _____

Employer: _____ Position: _____

Personal Reference: _____ Relationship: _____

Life ONLINE Rental applications request personal information. Be careful of scams!

G Match the red flag for online rental applications (left column) with the example (right column). **Life ONLINE**

____ 1. The price is too good to be true.   a. First and last month's rent, and a $3,000 security deposit will move you into the home of your dreams.

____ 2. The deposit is unusually high.   b. Send the deposit today to reserve this beautiful home. Then make an appointment to see it.

____ 3. There is a sad story.   c. Pay only $500 for this two-bedroom house for rent.

____ 4. You have to pay a deposit before you can see the home.   d. We must rent immediately because of a death in the family.

H APPLY Look online and find a rental application form. Share it with the class.

LESSON 4

We Need Furniture!

GOAL ▶ Identify rooms and furniture

A **INTERPRET** Read about the home Ernesto is going to rent. How many bedrooms and bathrooms does it have? How much is the rent?

FOR RENT

Three-bedroom, two-bathroom house with a big living room, a separate garage, a new remodeled kitchen, new washer/dryer, dishwasher, stove, and oven.
Utilities paid and no deposit required.
Rent: **$2,600** a month

Ask inside for more information

B Listen to the descriptions. Choose the description of Ernesto's new home.

Home 1   Home 2   Home 3   Home 4

C Complete the floor plan key with words from the box.

- bathroom
- ~~bedroom~~
- dining room
- kitchen
- living room
- yard

D Look at the floor plans. Which one is Ernesto's new home?

E Write the words under the furniture.

| armchair | coffee table | dining room table | end table |
| bookcase | couch | dresser | table lamp |

_____   _____   _____   _____
$950.89 $54.49 $669.89 $549.99

_____   _____   _____   _____
$875.00 $225.89 $275.99 $149.99

F **PLAN** Where would you put the furniture from E? Draw on the floor plan.

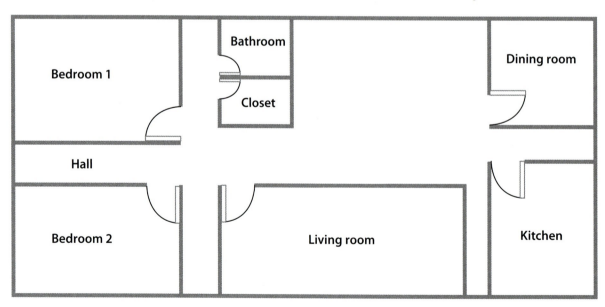

102   UNIT 4

G Study the photo with your classmates and teacher. Write the prepositions.

- The picture is _____ the couch.
- The lamp is _____ the end table.
- The fireplace is _____ the armchairs.
- The coffee table is _____ the couch.
- The coffee table is _____ the living room.
- The couch is _____ the coffee table.
- The couch is _____ the end table.
- The end table is _____ the corner.

H Practice the conversation with a partner. Make similar conversations using the furniture and floor plan in exercises **E** and **F**.

Student A: Where is the end table?

Student B: It's in the living room next to the couch.

I **CALCULATE** Decide what you want to buy and complete the invoice. Look at **E** for the prices.

McCarthy's Furniture Warehouse			
Quantity	Merchandise	Unit price	Total
1	couch	$950.89	$950.89
	armchair		
	end table		
	coffee table		
	table lamp		
	dining room table		
	dresser		
	bookcase		
		Total	

LESSON 4

LESSON 5: Family Budget

GOAL ▶ Make a family budget

A PREDICT Look at the picture. What are Ernesto and Virginia doing?

B INTERPRET Read about managing money and budgets. Underline any new words and look them up in a dictionary.

Be careful with your money. Follow these steps:
- Deposit your paycheck in the bank.
- Keep cash for emergencies.
- Only withdraw money from the bank when it is part of your budget.
- Don't use credit cards a lot. Use an ATM when you need cash.

Plan your budget. Follow these steps:
- Write down how much you need every month for rent, food, gas, water, and electricity.
- Write down how much you need to buy other things, like clothes.
- Plan how much money you need every month for entertainment.
- Plan how much you can put in your savings account for emergencies and for the future.

C Match each word with a definition. Write the correct word.

ATM	budget	cash	deposit	paycheck	withdraw

1. _____ put money in the bank
2. _____ a plan for your money
3. _____ take money out of the bank
4. _____ paper money and coins
5. _____ automated teller machine
6. _____ check received for work

D Study Ernesto and Virginia's family budget with your classmates and teacher.

Monthly Income	
Ernesto's wages	$3,000
Virginia's wages	$3,200
Total Income	
Monthly Expenses	
Rent	$2,600
Gas	
Electric	$125
Water	$70
Food	
Life insurance	$91
Auto insurance	$125
Gasoline	
Phone	
Credit cards	$300
Entertainment	
Clothing	$200
Household repairs	
Savings	$500
Taxes	$900
Total Expenses	

Wage and Salary
wage = amount of money based on hours worked
salary = fixed amount paid per year

E **CALCULATE** Listen and complete the budget. Then calculate the totals.

F Practice the conversation with a partner. Make new conversations using the information from the budget in D.

Student A: How much do they spend on water every month?

Student B: They spend about $70.

G Study the chart with your classmates and teacher.

Modal: *Might*			
Subject	Modal	Base verb	Example sentence
I / You / He / She / We / They	might	spend	We **might** spend $300 a month on food.

H **PLAN** Work with a partner. Imagine that you are a family. Make a budget. Write the information below.

Student A: How much do you think we spend on clothing each month?

Student B: We might spend $200.

Monthly Income	
_____	_____
_____	_____
Total Income	_____
Monthly Expenses	
_____	_____
_____	_____
_____	_____
_____	_____
_____	_____
_____	_____
_____	_____
_____	_____
_____	_____
_____	_____
_____	_____
_____	_____
_____	_____
Total Expenses	_____

LESSON 6
Explore the Workforce
GOAL ▶ Explore construction-related job opportunities

A INTERPRET Look at the chart and answer the questions.

1. Which career usually requires the most formal education?
2. What is the recommended education for a drafter?
3. How much money can an electrician earn in a year?
4. For inspectors, will there be more or fewer positions available in the future?

CONSTRUCTION CAREERS 2020

Job Title	Salary	Job Openings 2020	Job Outlook 2020-2030	Minimum Education
Architect	$82,320	126,700	3%	Bachelor's Degree
Inspector	$62,820	129,300	-3%	HS Diploma or Equivalent
Drafter	$57,960	191,800	-2%	Associate Degree
Plumber	$56,330	469,900	5%	HS Diploma or Equivalent
Electrician	$56,900	729,600	9%	HS Diploma or Equivalent
Carpenter	$49,520	942,900	2%	HS Diploma or Equivalent
Painter	$42,130	350,800	5%	No Formal Education
Woodworker	$33,750	247,100	8%	HS Diploma or Equivalent

Source Data: https://www.bls.gov

Information Question with *which*	Answer
Which career has the highest salary?	architect
Which careers might have fewer openings in the future?	inspector and drafter
Use *which* to ask the listener to choose from different choices.	

B Use the information in the chart and ask a partner questions to complete the table. Student A asks questions 1–3. Student B asks questions 4–6.

Example Questions:

According to the chart, which career...
    pays $56,330?
    had 729,600 openings?
    will have 9% more positions in the future?
    requires no formal education?

Career Title	Information
1.	$129,300
2.	$42,130
3.	2% more positions
4.	Bachelor's degree
5.	$191,800
6.	Associate degree

C Ask your partner additional questions about the chart using *which*.

D Read about training for a plumber position. What are three things you need to do to become a plumber?

> Most plumbers prepare for a plumbing career by doing an apprenticeship for four to five years. An apprenticeship is learning from an experienced worker, often on the job. Apprentice plumbers often receive 2,000 hours of paid work and some instruction. Most states require plumbers to get a license by taking an exam.

E Refer to A and D to answer the questions about training for a plumber job.

1. Do you think the pay is worth the time you need to train?
2. Do you think you could learn the skill it takes to do the work?
3. Do you like this kind of work?

F Read the job post. Check five things you think are most important.

PLUMBER'S APPRENTICE WANTED
Bixby Plumbing
Los Angeles, California
Apply **here**.

Job Type: Full-time
Benefits: Dental, Health, Vision Insurance
Salary: $35K–$44K per year
Required Experience: Experience preferred but not required

Qualities	You will learn to:
Good communication skills	bid on jobs
Works well with hands	plan work schedules
Good mechanical skills	talk to customers
Good troubleshooting skills	identify and use tools
	repair pipes
	identify problems and find solutions

Length of Apprenticeship

You will be prepared to take the exam for a plumber's license in as little as three years.

G Talk to a partner about a plumbing job. Do you think you could do the work?

H **REFLECT** Check what is true about you.

☐ I like working with my hands.　　☐ I am flexible.

☐ I like working by myself.　　☐ I like solving problems.

☐ I like working outside and inside.　　☐ I am detail-oriented.

☐ I like facts and information.　　☐ I am self-directed.

I **INVESTIGATE** In a group, follow the steps and research construction careers.

1. Go to your favorite search engine.
2. Type "construction careers."
3. Open at least three webpages.
4. Write five new things you learn.

1. _____
2. _____
3. _____
4. _____
5. _____

Workers talking at a construction site

LESSON 6　109

Review

A Complete the questions.

1. _____ kind of housing do you want?

2. _____ is the rent?

3. _____ house do you want, the three- or four-bedroom?

4. _____ is the condominium? Is it on Main Street?

5. _____ bedrooms does the apartment have?

B Scan the classified ads and answer the questions.

1. FOR RENT
Three-bedroom, two-bathroom condo with fireplace and air-conditioning.
Near schools and park.
Utilities included.
Rent: $2,550
Contact Agent

2. FOR RENT
Two-bedroom, two-bathroom with a fireplace, air-conditioning, a large garage, and a balcony.
Near public transportation.
Rent: $2,000 a month
Contact Agent

3. AVAILABLE
Large five-bedroom, three-bathroom house with a pool.
Near schools.
Rent: $3,400 a month
Contact Agent

4. FOR RENT
Two-bedroom, one-bathroom mobile home on a spacious lot.
Utilities included.
Rent: $2,250
Contact Agent

1. Which homes have a fireplace? _____

2. Which homes have utilities included? _____

3. Which home is less than $2,100? _____

4. Which homes have air-conditioning? _____

5. Which homes are near schools? _____

Learner Log	I can describe housing. ☐ Yes ☐ No ☐ Maybe	I can interpret classified ads. ☐ Yes ☐ No ☐ Maybe

C **Answer the questions.**

1. What is your present address? _____

2. What is your prior address? _____

3. What is your employer's name? _____

4. How many children live in your house? _____

5. Give one reference. _____

D **Write sentences about the location of furniture in the photo. Use prepositions.**

1. The fireplace is under the picture. _____

2. _____

3. _____

4. _____

5. _____

Learner Log   I can identify rooms and furniture.
☐ Yes ☐ No ☐ Maybe

Review

E Look at the rental application form. Where do you write the following information? Choose the correct answers.

RENTAL APPLICATION

1. Date: _____ 2. Name: _____
3. Present Address: _____
4. Prior Address: _____
5. Employer: _____
6. Position: _____
7. How many adults in unit: _____
8. How many children in unit: _____

1. June 3rd
   a. 1   b. 2   c. 5   d. 6

2. 8237 Henderson Park Rd.
   a. 2   b. 6   c. 4   d. 5

3. Sift Company
   a. 1   b. 3   c. 5   d. 6

F Look at the budget and write the answers.

Monthly Income	
Ernesto's wages	$3,000
Virginia's wages	$3,200
Total Income	
Monthly Expenses	
Rent	$1,200
Gas	$63
Electric	$125
Water	$70
Food	$1,100
Life insurance	$91
Auto insurance	$125
Total Expenses	

1. What is Ernesto's income?
   _____
2. How much is the apartment?
   _____
3. How much are the utilities?
   _____
4. What is the total income?
   _____
5. What are the total expenses?
   _____

Learner Log

I can complete a rental application form.
☐ Yes ☐ No ☐ Maybe

I can make a family budget.
☐ Yes ☐ No ☐ Maybe

Team Project

Plan a Move
SOFT SKILL ▶ Collaboration

Your team is a family that is going to move to a new home. Work together to plan the move.

1. Form a team of four or five students. In your team, you need:

Position	Job Description	Student Name
Student 1: **Team Leader**	Check that everyone speaks English. Check that everyone participates.	
Student 2: **Finance Planner**	Make a family budget with help from the team. Plan to pay rent and buy furniture.	
Student 3: **Writer**	Write a classified ad and fill out a rental application with help from the team.	
Students 4/5: **Decorators**	Buy and arrange furniture in the home with help from the team.	

2. Describe your family and the home you want. Write a classified ad for the home.
   - How many bedrooms do you need?
   - What kind of home do you need (house, condo, apartment)?
   - How much can you pay for rent?

3. Create a rental application and fill it out.

4. Make a family budget.

5. Make a list of the furniture you need and create an invoice for furniture.

6. Make a floor plan of the home and add the furniture.

7. Report to the class. Show the floor plan and classified ad.

   COLLABORATION
   Time Management
   You have limited time to complete the project. Plan your work first to make sure you will complete the project on time.

   Suggestions:
   1. **Work together** on every step of the project. Every step should be managed by different members. For example, the Financial Planner will manage writing the budget with help from everyone on the team.
   2. **Estimate** how much time your team has to complete the entire project.
   3. **Plan** how much time your team will take on each step of the project.
   4. **Assign** a timekeeper, who can be the Team Leader, to make sure you don't get behind in your work.

Reading Challenge

A Work in a group. Imagine you just arrived in the United States. What do you need to do first? Number the activities in order of when you will do them. 1 = *first*.

_____ Get housing

_____ Find schooling

_____ Buy furniture

_____ Find help from friends, family, or government agencies

_____ Find a place to sleep the first night

_____ Find food to eat

_____ Find a job

_____ Learn English

B Look at the words. Use a dictionary and match each word with the correct definition.

_____ 1. refugees   a. Money or things people give away to other people who need them

_____ 2. donations   b. People who leave their country because they are in danger from war or from the results of natural disasters

_____ 3. volunteers   c. People who give their time with no pay to help others

C Read the text and underline the words you don't know.

D Answer the questions about the text.

1. Who provides the refugee with $1,000? _____

2. Who helps the refugee with a housing payment? _____

3. How does the boy in the story feel about the refugees? _____

E In a group, discuss these questions. Then write the line number(s) that helped you decide.

1. How do you know the volunteer is happy with her son? Line _____

2. How do you know how the son feels about the volunteer work and the refugee? Line _____

3. How do you know the boy wants more information? Line _____

F Maybe the volunteer is happy because her son wants to help people. Think of three people you help or could help. In your notebook, write what you could do for them.

Refugees celebrate during a Refugee Birthday Party at the Della Lamb Community Center in Kansas City, Missouri.

Helping Neighbors

A 19-year-old refugee from Afghanistan arrives in the United States, and the government supplies $1,000 for his first three months. That is not a lot of money to live on. Fortunately, Della Lamb Community Services in Kansas City, Missouri, finds him housing and pays for his first and last month's rent through donations. Della Lamb helps
5 refugees from other countries, like these teenage boys. They are refugees from Uganda. On this day, they were in a birthday celebration for refugees that Della Lamb organized.

Della Lamb is completely run and operated by volunteers. The many volunteers have special experiences that help form a strong community. This is a comment from one volunteer: "I had my son with me and it was such a great experience for him…
10 it was a great exercise in looking at unit prices, generic brands,* and balancing the amount we had to spend while reminding ourselves of the overall objective* (to get them set up with basics in the house and enough food for a week, etc.). He asked me so many questions! He wanted to know if we would be able to meet them, what happens after they move in, do they speak English, how do they get jobs, and much
15 more. He was very concerned about them! Very sweet.

The best part was when he said, 'Next time we do this, we'll…' My heart!"

---

generic brands products from a company that doesn't advertise (they are usually cheaper)
objective goal

Too Good to Be True?

You cannot tell how big a place is from photos. Always visit a property you want to rent or buy to make sure it fits your needs.

Before You Watch

A **Choose the types of communication you have received.**

☐ A phone call with a recorded message.   ☐ An email saying you won a prize.

☐ A text from someone you don't know.   ☐ A text message with a link.

☐ An email IN ALL CAPS.   ☐ An online ad with very low prices.

B **Complete the sentences with words from the box.**

report	scam	trick you into	urgent

1. One type of _____ is when somebody tries to _____ giving them money for an apartment that isn't real.

2. When you tell a person in charge about a problem, you _____ the problem.

3. Something _____ is very important and you must do something about it right away.

C This video is about scams and how to avoid them. What advice do you think you will hear?

While You Watch

D Watch the video. Choose the things you hear.

☐ classified ads ☐ texts ☐ library books

☐ phone calls ☐ online videos ☐ emails

☐ social media ☐ online ads ☐ letters in the mail

E Read the sentences and watch the video again. Choose the signs of a scam.

☐ Someone you don't know asks you for personal information.

☐ A landlord asks for money before you see an apartment.

☐ Your friend texts you a link to a funny video.

☐ Your bank sends an email asking you to contact them.

☐ An email has misspelled words and words in all caps.

☐ An email address doesn't match the sender's name.

After You Watch

F Read each sentence. Choose *T* if it is true and *F* if it is false.

1. Sometimes scammers pretend to be from companies you know. T F
2. Scams always happen on the phone. T F
3. You should never click a link that a stranger texts you. T F
4. You should always do some research before you send money. T F
5. You should pay your rent with gift cards. T F

G With a partner, write three types of scams you remember from the video. Then talk about how you can protect yourself from these scams.

_____

_____

5 Our Community

UNIT OUTCOMES

▸ Describe your community
▸ Scan websites and search results
▸ Give and follow directions
▸ Read a message or letter
▸ Write and send a letter or email
▸ Identify employment in public safety careers

Look at the photo and answer the questions.

1. Where do you think this is?
2. What do you see?

This photo is the Annual Block party in Brooklyn, New York.

1. What do you think a block party is?
2. How does this block party create a sense of community?
3. How does this community event compare to events where you live?
4. How many people are dancing? What is everyone else doing?
5. Do you think these people know each other?

119

LESSON 1

Getting Around Town
GOAL ▶ Describe your community

A INTERPRET Read the Palm City web page. Make a list of other things you might find in the southeast.

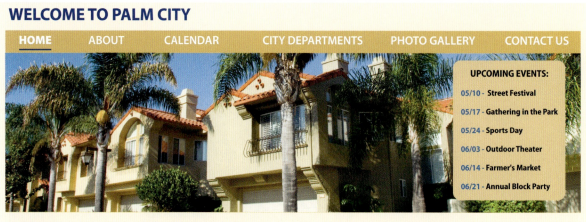

WELCOME TO PALM CITY

HOME   ABOUT   CALENDAR   CITY DEPARTMENTS   PHOTO GALLERY   CONTACT US

UPCOMING EVENTS:
05/10 - Street Festival
05/17 - Gathering in the Park
05/24 - Sports Day
06/03 - Outdoor Theater
06/14 - Farmer's Market
06/21 - Annual Block Party

ABOUT
Our small planned community is perfect for family life. Enjoy a central park in the middle of the city. Beautiful homes and schools are in the northwest. The Palm City Mall has over 100 stores and is in the northeast. Spend your weekends at Valley Entertainment Center in the southeast. There is a bowling alley, a movie theater, an arcade, and much more. City Hall and many public services are in the southwest part of town. We have planned it so the bus circles our town in exactly one hour.

B Read the web page again and complete the chart.

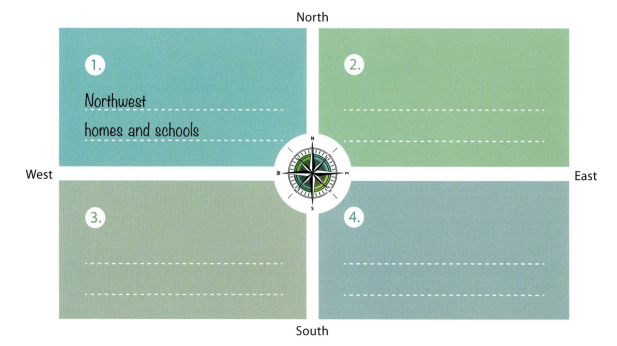

North

1. Northwest
homes and schools

2.

West   East

3.

4.

South

120   UNIT 5

C ANALYZE Look at the bus schedule. Write the names of the streets on the map.

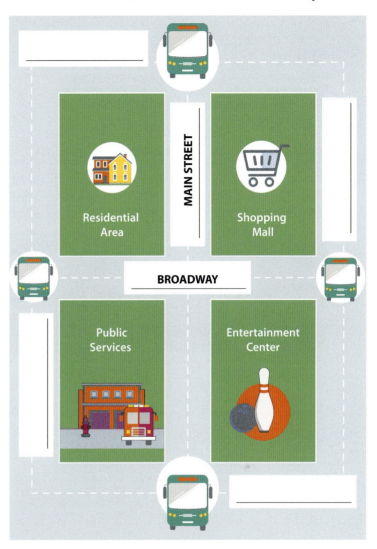

Information Questions				
Question Word		Subject	Base Verb	
When	does	the bus	stop	in the residential area?
Where				

D Practice the conversations. Use the information in C to make new conversations.

Student A: When does the bus stop in the residential area?

Student B: It stops at 7:00 a.m.

Student B: Where does the bus stop at 8:45?

Student A: It stops at public services.

LESSON 1 121

E CLASSIFY Read the words and write them in the correct columns. Then listen and check your answers.

apartment	courthouse	hardware store	pharmacy
bank	department store	hospital	police station
city hall	fast-food restaurant	~~house~~	post office
clothes store	fire station	library	shoe store
condominium	gas station	mobile home	supermarket

Residential	Public Services	Retail

house _____ _____
_____ _____ _____
_____ _____ _____
_____ _____ _____
          _____ _____
          _____ _____
          _____ _____

F List places in your community that are close to your home.

LESSON 2 What's the Number?

GOAL ▶ Scan websites and search results

A PREDICT Look at the website. Circle the search icon.

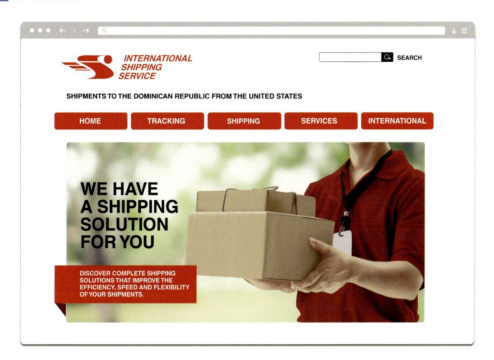

B Read the paragraph. What is the problem and the solution?

> Marie lives in Palm City. She wants to send a gift to her friend in the Dominican Republic. She needs to learn how to send a package to her friend. She goes to the website of an international shipping company to find out. She looks at the page and finally decides to click on the "International" tab. If she doesn't see the information she wants, she can always click the search icon.

C Choose the correct answers.

1. What does Marie want to do?
   a. She wants to get insurance.
   b. She wants to travel to the Dominican Republic.
   c. She wants to send a package.

2. What does Marie click on the home page?
   a. She clicks on the search icon.
   b. She clicks on the "International" tab.
   c. She clicks on the "Home" tab.

LESSON 2   123

D INTERPRET Scan the Palm City Directory. Circle any words you don't know.

PALM CITY DIRECTORY

HOME | ABOUT | CALENDAR | **BUSINESS DIRECTORY** | PHOTO GALLERY | CONTACT US

DIRECTORY

Art Galleries	Museums
Attorneys	Post Office
Banks	Real Estate Agencies
Churches	Rental Cars
Community Services	Restaurants
Libraries	Retail
Playgrounds and Parks	Schools (private)
Dentists	Schools (public)
Department Stores	Transportation
Doctors	Bus Lines
Furniture	Shuttle Service
Grocery Stores	Taxis
Home Improvement	Train
Hospital	Travel Agencies

E INTERPRET Write the links that will help Marie find locations in Palm City. Complete the table.

Marie needs …	Link
to send a package.	Post Office
to buy food.	
a new sweater.	
a taxi to the airport.	
to find a place to go for dinner.	
to repair a broken window.	
to see a lawyer.	

Simple Present	
Subject	**Verb**
I / You / We / They	need, want
He / She / It	needs, wants

F INTERPRET Study the directory with your classmates and teacher.

Palm City Government Agencies and Services

City Hall 160 W. Broadway Ave.	(520) 555-3300	**Angel Park** 137 Monroe St.	(520) 555-3224
Courthouse 150 W. Broadway Ave.	(520) 555-5245	**Lilly Community Park** 275 Carpenter St.	(520) 555-2211

DMV (Department of Motor Vehicles)
375 Western Ave.
  Information
  Appointments
	
	(520) 555-2227
	(520) 555-2778
		Police Department
		Emergencies call 911
		140 W. Broadway Ave.
			(520) 555-4867

Fire Department **Emergencies call 911** 145 W. Broadway Ave.	(520) 555-3473	**Schools (Public)**	
		Jefferson Middle 122 Jefferson St.	(520) 555-2665
Library (Public) 125 E. Broadway Ave.	(520) 555-7323	**Lincoln High** 278 Lincoln Ave.	(520) 555-8336
Playgrounds and Parks		**Washington Elementary** 210 Washington St.	(520) 555-5437
Department of Parks and Recreation 160 W. Broadway Ave. Suite 15	(520) 555-7275	**US Post Office** 151 E. Broadway Ave.	(520) 555-6245

G Listen and practice the conversation. Then ask a partner for information about the *post office, courthouse, DMV, fire department, City Hall,* and *Jefferson Middle School.*

Student A: Where's the post office?
Student B: It's at 151 East Broadway Avenue.
Student A: What's the phone number?
Student B: It's (520) 555-6245.

H CLASSIFY Cover the directory and listen to the conversations. Write the places, addresses, and phone numbers you hear in the table.

Place	Address	Phone
1.		
2.		
3.		
4.		
5.		

I APPLY What are the most important phone numbers to have? Make a list with a group.

LESSON 2

LESSON 3 Finding Your Way
GOAL ▶ Give and follow directions

A INTERPRET Look at the map and practice the conversation. Make new conversations with other places on the map.

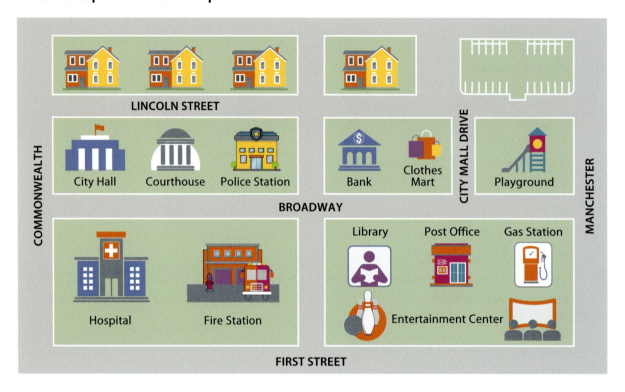

Student A: Where is the bank?

Student B: It's on Broadway.

B Study the prepositions with your classmates and teacher.

next to   on the corner of   between   across from

126   UNIT 5

C Look at the map in **A**. Complete the sentences with prepositions.

1. The gas station is _____ Broadway and Manchester.
2. The courthouse is _____ City Hall and the police station.
3. The post office is _____ the library.
4. The police station is _____ the fire station.
5. City Hall is _____ the hospital.
6. The post office is _____ the library and the gas station.

D Study the chart with your classmates and teacher.

Imperatives			
	Base Verb		Example Sentence
you	go	straight straight ahead	**Go** straight three blocks. **Go** straight ahead.
	turn	left right around	**Turn** left on Nutwood. **Turn** right on Nutwood. **Turn** around.
	stop	on the left on the right	**Stop** on the left. **Stop** on the right.

E Listen to the conversation between Marie and her friend. Find Marie's apartment on the map and circle it.

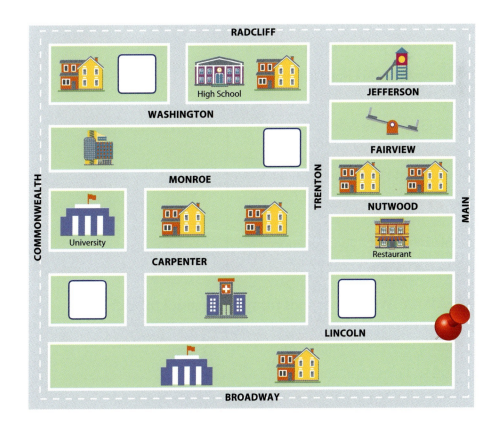

LESSON 3

F Listen to the directions. Follow the map in E and write the location.

G Look at the map in E again. Start at the red pin and write directions to the high school.

The high school: _____

_____

_____

_____

H Write directions to the restaurant and the university. Start at the red pin.

_____

_____

_____

_____

Life ONLINE Map programs online or apps on smartphones have many special features that can help you find your location faster. For example, often at the bottom of the directions to a store or another place of business, the app will include the phone number and the website of the location you are looking for.

I Draw lines to the special features of this map program.

1. Reverse directions to find your way home

2. Choose the time you want to arrive, or you want to leave.

3. Choose the transportation you want to take or if you want to walk.

4. Enter your home address into the app or program.

J **APPLY** Write directions from your school to your home.

_____

_____

_____

128 UNIT 5

LESSON 4

Dear Raquel
GOAL ▶ Read a message or letter

A Read Marie's email to her friend Raquel in the Dominican Republic.

> Dear Raquel,
>
> How are you? I'm fine and happy. I miss the DR. I miss you too. How's everyone? I have a new job now and I really like it. I'm a nurse assistant at St. Michael's Hospital here in Palm City. I'm also studying English at the adult school.
>
> Palm City is a nice community. There's a park on the corner near the hospital. I eat my lunch there. City Hall and the courthouse are across from the hospital. My apartment is on the corner of Washington and Wilson. I live about four blocks from the hospital.
>
> I sometimes go to the mall at night. I eat dinner at a restaurant on Main Street or across the street at the coffee shop. I hope you can visit soon. There are lots of things we can do at night after work. I attached a picture of me in the hospital.
>
> Your friend,
>
> Marie
>
>

 Attachments like pictures or documents can be dangerous to download. Never download any attachment or click on any link from an email unless you know the sender.

B Answer the questions in complete sentences. Use prepositions.

1. Where does Marie eat lunch? Where is it?

   She eats lunch in the park. It's on the corner near the hospital.

2. Where does Marie work? Where is the building?

   _____

3. Where is the courthouse?

   _____

4. Where does Marie eat dinner? Where is the building?

   _____

C Study the charts with your classmates and teacher.

Simple Present	
Subject	Verb
I / You / We / They	eat.
He / She / It	eats.

Simple Present: Be		
Subject	Be	
I	am	happy. sad. tired.
You / We / They	are	
He / She / It	is	

Present Continuous			
Subject	Be	Base Verb + ing	Example Sentence
I	am	writing	I **am** / I**'m writing** this letter in English.
You / We / They	are	going	We **are** / We**'re going** to the mall.
He / She / It	is	eating	He **is** / He**'s eating** at the coffee shop.

D Read the email from Raquel to her friend. Circle the simple present verbs. Underline the present continuous verbs.

> Dear Judy,
>
> I'm writing to you from Palm City in Arizona. I'm staying for a few days with my friend, Marie. I'm having a wonderful time. Palm City is beautiful. People are very friendly. We are going to Claudia's Restaurant to eat Mexican food tonight.
>
> Marie works in the hospital here as a nurse. She goes to work early every day, and she works very hard. She loves her new job, but she's a little sad because her family and friends aren't here.
>
> Right now, I'm doing my English homework and listening to music at Marie's house because I'm waiting for her to finish work. Wish you were here!
>
> Love,
>
> Raquel

E **INFER** On a piece of paper, answer the questions in complete sentences.

1. Is Raquel happy or sad?
2. What does Marie do every day?
3. What is Raquel doing right now?
4. Is Marie happy or sad?

F PREDICT Read the questions and predict the answers. Then listen to the email from Raquel to her friend Judy, and check your answers.

1. How is the weather in Palm City?

    a. cold   b. warm   c. hot

2. Where does the bus stop?

    a. near the park   b. near the shopping mall   c. near Marie's house

3. What are in the parks?

    a. palm trees and cactus plants   b. children   c. tables

G APPLY On a separate piece of paper, write sentences about the city where you live.

1. Where do you live? What is the name of your town or city?

2. Describe your city. Is it beautiful, crowded, old, new, big, or small?

3. How is the weather in your city? Is the weather cold, warm, or hot most of the time?

4. Where do you like to go in your city? Do you like to go to stores, restaurants, entertainment places, or parks?

H CREATE Complete the email with your sentences from G.

Dear _____,

I hope you are well. I'm fine. I live in _____. It is _____

_____

_____

_____

_____

_____

_____

_____

_____

LESSON 4

LESSON 5	**The City Is Beautiful!**
	GOAL ▶ Write and send a letter or email

A **CLASSIFY** Read the envelope and complete the table.

Raquel Abreu
133 Washington Street #15
Palm City, AZ 85193

Antonio Abreu
18 Calle Mozart
Santo Domingo 10413
Republica Dominicana

From:		To:	
Street:		Street:	
City:		City:	
Zip code:		Zip code:	
State:		State:	
Country:		Country:	

B Complete the envelope from you to a partner's address.

132   UNIT 5

C Study the parts of a letter. Then listen to a lecture and number the parts.

Parts of a letter	Example
_____ body	most of the information
_____ closing	Sincerely, Love, Love always, Your friend,
_____ closing sentence	Call me! I hope to see you soon.
_1_ date	January 20th
_____ purpose or reason	I am writing because . . .
_____ greeting	Dear Raquel,
_____ your name	first name, or first and last name

D **SEQUENCE** Read the parts of the letter and put them in the correct order. Write the correct number next to each part. What do you write in a letter, but not an email?

a. _____ I'll call you tomorrow.

b. _1_ March 12th

c. _____ This city is wonderful. The weather is warm most of the time. There are many parks, stores, and restaurants. There's good bus service. The bus goes around the city in an hour and stops near the shopping mall. The shopping mall has over a hundred stores, and I go there every day. The parks are very beautiful. There are a lot of palm trees and cactus plants.

d. _____ Dear Judy,

e. _____ Raquel

f. _____ I am writing to tell you that I am staying with Marie in Palm City for one more week. I am having a lot of fun. Marie is very nice and kind. We went to the mall last night. Today, we walked in the park on her lunch break.

g. _____ Love,

LESSON 5 133

E Study the charts with your classmates and teacher.

Simple Past (Regular)		
Subject	Verb (Base + *ed*)	Example Sentence
I / You / He / She / It / We / They	talked	I **talked** with Marie.
	wanted	She **wanted** a sandwich.
	walked	We **walked** in the park.

Simple Past (Irregular)		
Subject	Irregular Verb	Example Sentence
I / You / He / She / It / We / They	went (go)	I **went** to the park.
	ate (eat)	She **ate** at the coffee shop.
	bought (buy)	We **bought** new dresses.
	sent (send)	They **sent** a letter.

F Complete each sentence with the past form of the verb in parentheses.

1. I _____ (walk) to Marie's house.

2. You _____ (go) to school yesterday.

3. She _____ (send) me a letter from Palm City.

4. I _____ (want) a new sweater.

5. Raquel and Marie _____ (buy) new clothes at the store.

6. We _____ (eat) at the restaurant on the corner of Main and Carpenter.

G **APPLY** Complete the sentences for yourself.

1. My city is _____.

2. There is a _____.

3. Every day, I _____.

4. Sometimes, I _____.

5. Yesterday, I _____.

6. Yesterday, I _____.

H Write an email and send it to a classmate.

LESSON 6: Explore the Workforce

GOAL ▶ Identify employment in public safety careers

A **INFER** Look at the infographic and give your opinion.

1. Which job do you think is easiest to get?
2. Do you think that a security guard makes enough money to support a family of four?
3. Why do you think police officers make more than the other workers?
4. Do you think you need special education or training to be a paramedic?

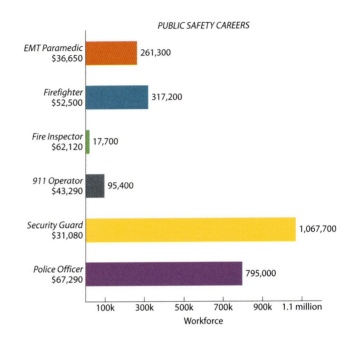

Comparatives / Superlatives (Count Nouns)
Which careers have *more* workers in the workforce *than* firefighters?
Which career has *the most* workers in the workforce?
Which careers have *fewer* workers in the workforce *than* firefighters?
Which career has *the fewest* workers in the workforce?

B Use the information in **A** and complete the chart.

Career with Fewest Workers ⟶ Career with Most Workers

C Ask your partner questions about the chart in **B**.

Example Questions:

Which career has the fewest workers in the United States?

Which careers have more workers than fire inspectors?

LESSON 6   135

D Read about a firefighter career.

> Firefighting can be dangerous. Firefighters have to go into buildings that are on fire, give medical assistance, and respond to emergencies regularly. They often do other duties when waiting for a call. Their shifts can be 24 hours at a time, so many times they have to eat and sleep in the firehouse. Firefighters must also be strong and in good health.

E **INFER** Discuss the questions about firefighters based on the reading in D.

1. Do you think firefighters have to exercise?
2. Do you think firefighters work five days a week and have weekends off?
3. Do you think a firefighter's work is more dangerous than a police officer's work?

F Read the information. Look up words you don't know in the dictionary.

Firefighters have to be ready for anything. They have to be strong to carry or move heavy objects and people.

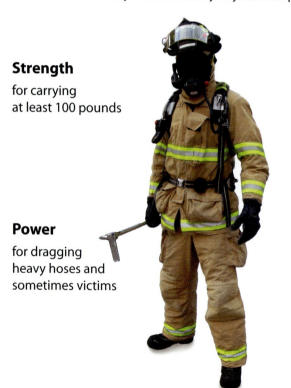

Strength
for carrying at least 100 pounds

Power
for dragging heavy hoses and sometimes victims

Cardiovascular Fitness
for working in difficult places where it is hard to breathe and where there is a lot of stress

Core and Back Strength
for avoiding injury because of hard physical work

Flexibility
for crawling and getting into tight places

G This firefighter is working to control a fire in the Shasta-Trinity National Forest in California. Think about his job. Talk to a partner about it. Do you think you could do the work?

H **REFLECT** Check what is true about you.

☐ I am enthusiastic about life. ☐ I think on my feet. (I come up with solutions quickly.)

☐ I like working in a team. ☐ I like solving problems.

☐ I like working outside. ☐ I like physical work.

☐ I learn best by doing things. ☐ I don't have a problem with change.

I **INVESTIGATE** In a group, follow the steps and research public safety careers.

1. Go to your favorite search engine.

2. Type "public safety careers."

3. Open at least three webpages.

4. Write five new things you learn.

1. _____

2. _____

3. _____

4. _____

5. _____

J Choose a job or career related to public safety. Go to a job search site online and see if there are any openings within 25 miles of your school or home.

LESSON 6

Review

A Read the directions and follow the routes on the map. Write the names of the places where you arrive.

| bank | hospital | library | pharmacy | post office |

1. You are at the intersection of Union and Mason. Go east on Union for two blocks. Then turn left. It's on the right. _____

2. You are at the intersection of Chestnut and Powell. Go south on Powell for one block. Then go west on Lombard one block. It is across the street. _____

3. You are at the intersection of Green and Mason. Go west on Green for four blocks. Then go north one block. It's on the corner. _____

4. You are at the intersection of Montgomery and Vallejo. Go west on Vallejo for three blocks and turn left. Go one block. It's on the right. _____

5. You are at the intersection of Broadway and Powell. Go south on Powell. Go two blocks and turn left. It's on the right. _____

Learner Log   I can give and follow directions.
☐ Yes   ☐ No   ☐ Maybe

B Answer the questions.

1. Where can you send a package? _____
2. Where can you borrow a book? _____
3. Where can you buy gas for your car? _____
4. Where can you buy medicine? _____
5. Where can you eat a burger and french fries? _____
6. Where can you find a doctor? _____
7. Where can you report a crime? _____
8. Where can you register the birth of a new baby? _____

C Read the paragraph. Complete the sentences with the correct form of the verb *be*.

This city _____ wonderful. The weather _____ warm most of the time. There _____ many parks, stores, and restaurants. There _____ good bus service. The bus goes around the city in an hour and stops near the shopping mall. There _____ over a hundred stores in the shopping mall, and I go there every day. The parks _____ very beautiful. There _____ a lot of palm trees and beautiful flowers.

D Read the email. Circle the correct form of the verbs.

Dear Roberto,

I (write / am writing) to you from Connecticut. I (sit / am sitting) on the beach. I (stay / am staying) here in Clinton with my friend Suzanna. It's very warm and sunny here in summer. We (walk / are walking) on the beach every day. We often (eat / are eating) Mexican food in the evening. On weekends, we (visit / are visiting) beautiful places along the coast.

Is it warm in Texas? I hope you (have / are having) a nice vacation there.

Your friend,

Sara

Learner Log

I can describe my community.
☐ Yes ☐ No ☐ Maybe

I can read a message or letter.
☐ Yes ☐ No ☐ Maybe

Review

E Write down important business locations in your neighborhood. Look up their phone numbers online and add them to your list.

Location	Phone Number

F Complete the profile and write a paragraph about what you did yesterday.

NAME:
CITY:
STATE:

POSTS
INFORMATION
PHOTOS
FRIEND LIST

YESTERDAY
_____
_____
_____
_____
_____
_____

Learner Log

I can scan websites and search results.
☐ Yes ☐ No ☐ Maybe

I can write and send a letter or email.
☐ Yes ☐ No ☐ Maybe

Team Project

Describe Your Community
SOFT SKILL ▶ Presentation Skills

In a group, you are going to describe your community and write an email to a friend.

1. Form a team with four or five students. In your team, you need:

Position	Job Description	Student Name
Student 1: **Team Leader**	Check that everyone speaks English. Check that everyone participates.	
Student 2: **Writer**	Write a paragraph about your community with help from the team.	
Student 3: **Artist**	Make a map of your community with help from the team.	
Students 4/5: **Spokespeople**	Prepare a class presentation with help from the team.	

2. Draw a map of the community around your school. Think about these questions: What buildings are there? What are the names of the streets? Is there a city bus? Where does it stop?

3. Write a paragraph about your community. Then write an email to a friend. Invite him or her to visit you.

4. Present your work to the class.

   PRESENTATION SKILLS
   Presenters
   1. Organize and practice in your group first.
   2. Stand in presentation order.
   3. Have a visual for your part of the presentation. For example, in this project you have a map, a paragraph, and a postcard.
   4. Make eye contact.
   5. Speak clearly and loud enough that people can hear.

   Audience
   Rate the presenters. Use this rubric.

Organization	Visuals	Eye Contact	Voice Loud Enough
not organized	no visuals	No member makes eye contact.	No member speaks loudly enough.
Some members know their parts.	cannot see visuals	Some members make eye contact.	Some members speak loudly enough.
Everyone knows their part.	can see all visuals	All members make eye contact.	All members speak loudly enough.

Reading Challenge

A In this unit, we practiced describing a community, but is a community more than streets and buildings? Look up the definition of community in the dictionary and write it.

_____

_____

_____

B In a group, discuss what makes a strong community. Write a few words that help describe what a strong community is.

_____   _____

_____   _____

C Read the title of the reading on the next page. How do you think someone could build a community?

D Read the text on the next page. Underline words that you don't know.

E Answer the questions about the text. Write the line where you find the answer.

1. Where did Jaime get a high school diploma? Line _____

2. What is the name of the business Jaime started? Line _____

3. Where is the business? Line _____

4. When is the marketplace open? Line _____

F **INFER** Look at the words from the reading. Guess their meaning without looking them up in the dictionary.

1. _____ diverse   a. street market that sells clothes, food, and other things

2. _____ swap meet   b. from many different places

G Work in a group. Give the group your opinion about the questions. Cite your evidence from the reading.

1. Do you think people in Hillsboro are from many different countries?

2. Do you think Jaime's family had a really good life when they lived in Mexico?

3. Do you think M&M Marketplace wants business from people of many different countries?

H Work in a group. Discuss the benefits of having a strong community.

Building Community in Hillsboro

Jaime Miranda, an immigrant from Mexico, grew up in Mexico City. His family migrated to the United States when he was nine years old, looking for a better life. They ended up in Oregon, where he was the first member of his family to get a high school diploma and attend college. He started a business in Hillsboro.

5   Hillsboro is a city of just over 100,000 people and is one of the most racially **diverse** communities in Oregon. People of all kinds make up the community. The Hillsboro website reads: "…big cities and large institutions don't necessarily produce *greatness*; people do."

Jaime decided to help other immigrants build their own businesses by starting a
10 local **swap meet** called M&M Marketplace. It started with 20 businesses and, in just over 20 years, has grown to 80. Now the marketplace is open every weekend and has sports, entertainment, and recreation for all ages.

The website for M&M Marketplace reads: "…we want to invite people of all cultures and nationalities to be part of our market, thus contributing to our growth and
15 cultural diversity."

Fruit cups are a popular snack sold at the M&M Marketplace.

6 Health

UNIT OUTCOMES

- Describe healthy practices
- Identify illnesses
- Make a doctor's appointment
- Read medicine labels
- Identify and describe emergencies
- Explore careers in the medical field

Look at the photo and answer the questions.

1. Where are these people? What are they doing?
2. What are some benefits of exercise?

A group of construction and iron workers stretch and bend before their workday starts at Exempla Good Samaritan Medical Center in Lafayette, Colorado.

1. This morning workout has helped these workers avoid accidents for almost a year. Why do you think this is?
2. What are these people wearing? Why?
3. Do you think it's easy to stretch in these clothes?

LESSON 1

A Healthy Life

GOAL ▶ Describe healthy practices

A Match the statements with the photos. Write *a*, *b*, *c*, or *d*.

_____ 1. How much sleep you need changes as you age. How many hours of sleep do you think adults and children need?

a.

_____ 2. Some experts are sounding an alarm about screen time outside of work. How much screen time do you think people should have outside of work?

b.

_____ 3. The amount of physical activity adults need depends on whether they want to lose weight, maintain weight, or meet fitness goals. How much exercise do adults need a day?

c.

_____ 4. Many people become emotional, frustrated, or nervous because of stress and anxiety. What can people do about stress?

d.

B **SURVEY** Work in a group. Discuss the questions in **A** and complete the sentences.

1. We think that adults need _____ hours of exercise a week.

2. We think that adults should have no more than _____ hours of screen time outside of work.

3. Our class thinks stress is when people worry a lot. We think people can _____
   _____.

4. We think adults need _____ hours of sleep every night. We think that children need _____ hours of sleep a night.

C PREDICT Look at the photo. What is the man's problem? What can he do?

D Read about stress. Define the words *treatments* and *symptoms* in line 3.

> 1 Many people have stress. Stress can make people tired, it can make them lose
> 2 sleep, it can cause problems like *high blood pressure*, and it can even cause heart
> 3 problems. There are treatments for the symptoms of stress! Doctors say that exercise,
> 4 a balanced diet, meditation, and rest can help. Exercise and a good diet help people
> 5 to think more clearly and have more energy. When people exercise, they sleep
> 6 better, too.
>
> **high blood pressure** health condition that can cause problems like heart disease

E CLASSIFY Complete the table about stress.

| balanced diet | heart problems | lose sleep | rest |
| exercise | high blood pressure | meditation | tired |

Symptoms	Remedies (Cures)

F IDENTIFY Read the list below in a group. Check (✓) the healthy practices.

- ☐ eat three meals a day
- ☐ sleep twelve hours
- ☐ work twelve hours a day
- ☐ smoke
- ☐ exercise every day
- ☐ play sports
- ☐ eat a lot of candy
- ☐ drink alcohol regularly
- ☐ rest and take breaks

G **PREDICT** Guess the missing information. Then listen to the lecture and check your answers.

1. Doctors say adults need to exercise _____ minutes a _____.

2. Doctors say adults need to eat _____ balanced meals a day.

3. Doctors say all adults need to go in for a checkup _____ time(s) a _____.

4. Doctors say we should not _____.

5. Doctors say we should take _____.

habit something a person does every day
vitamin pill or liquid containing things to keep the body healthy

H Read the questions and choose the answers for yourself.

1. Are you tired during the day?   Yes   No
2. Do you need more sleep?   Yes   No
3. Do you have a balanced diet?   Yes   No
4. Do you take vitamins?   Yes   No
5. Do you have a checkup every year?   Yes   No

Infinitives		
Subject	**Verb**	*to* + **Base Verb**
I	need	to exercise.

I **APPLY** Write your health goals.

EXAMPLE: I need to exercise 30 minutes every day.

_____
_____
_____
_____

LESSON 2

What's the Matter?
GOAL ▶ Identify illnesses

A IDENTIFY Look at the photo and write the words.

| arm(s) | ear(s) | foot (feet) | head | mouth | nose | stomach |
| chest | eye(s) | hand(s) | leg(s) | neck | shoulder(s) | |

B Practice the conversation. Make new conversations using the words in **A**.

Student A: What's the matter?　　　　**Student A:** What's wrong?

Student B: My <u>head</u> hurts.　　　　**Student B:** My <u>arms</u> hurt.

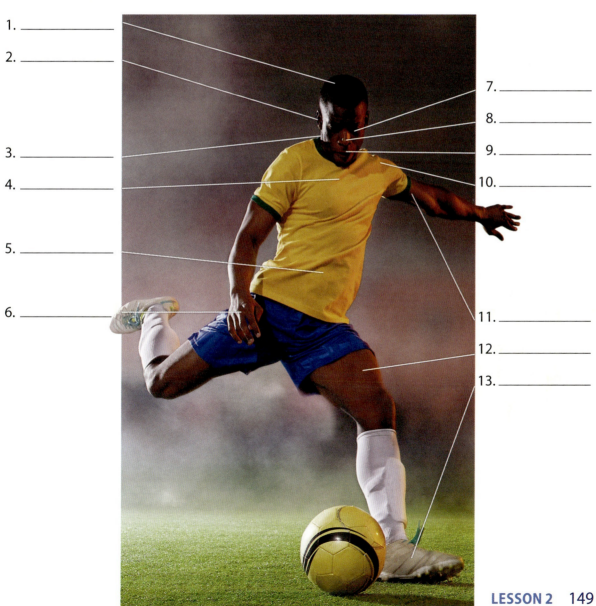

1. _____
2. _____
3. _____
4. _____
5. _____
6. _____
7. _____
8. _____
9. _____
10. _____
11. _____
12. _____
13. _____

C Write the words under the photos. Then listen and write the number of the conversation above each picture. 🎧

| cough | fever | headache | runny nose | sore throat |

____ ____ ____ ____ ____

_____ _____ _____ _____ _____

D Read. Use a dictionary to find the meaning of any new words. 🎧

> A cold and the flu are similar illnesses and have some of the same symptoms. The symptoms of a cold are a low fever, a sore throat, a headache, and a runny nose. People usually have a cold for one or two weeks. People with the flu feel very tired and sick. They often have a high fever, a dry cough, a headache, and muscle aches. Just like a cold, people can have the flu for one or two weeks. Many people get a cold or the flu every year and hate them both!

E **CLASSIFY** Compare cold and flu symptoms. Complete the table.

Cold Symptoms	Flu Symptoms

150 UNIT 6

F Study the chart with your classmates and teacher.

Adjective	Comparative Adjective	Superlative Adjective
serious	more serious less serious	the most serious the least serious
common	more common less common	the most common the least common

G **RANK** Work in a group. Look at the illnesses and symptoms. Rank them from *1* to *8*. Rank the most serious as *1*.

1. _____ a backache
2. _____ a cold
3. _____ a headache
4. _____ a runny nose
5. _____ a sore throat
6. _____ a stomachache
7. _____ a toothache
8. _____ the flu

H **LIST** Work in a group. Make a list of illnesses and symptoms that you think are the most common.

_____
_____
_____
_____
_____
_____

LESSON 2 151

LESSON 3: Making an Appointment

GOAL ▶ Make a doctor's appointment

A Read. What is the problem and a solution?

> My name is Yasir. I'm from Somalia. I like school and I want to learn English, but I don't go to class very much. I'm tired a lot. I need to see a doctor, but I'm very nervous because I don't speak English well. My teacher says the doctor can help me feel better. Maybe I can bring a friend to help me.

B Study the charts with your classmates and teacher.

Simple Past (Regular)	
Subject	Verb (Base + *ed*)
I / You	walked.* (walk)
He / She / It	talked.* (talk)
We / They	smoked.* (smoke) played.* (play) waited.* (wait)

Simple Past (Irregular)	
Subject	Verb
I / You	had. (have)
He / She / It	went. (go)
We / They	said. (say)

*See the pronunciation note.

Simple Past: *Be*		
Subject	Be	Example Sentence
I / He / She / It	was	I **was** sick.
You / We / They	were	You **were** at the hospital.

Past Tense
Notice how we pronounce the end sound when speaking about the past.
/t/ = walk/t/, talk/t/, smoke/t/
/d/ = play/d/
/ɪd/ = wait/ɪd/

C Listen to Yasir. Match the two parts of each sentence.

_____ 1. He was   a. to smoke.
_____ 2. He went   b. to the doctor.
_____ 3. The doctor said   c. to stop smoking.
_____ 4. He continued   d. a heart attack.
_____ 5. He had   e. tired a lot.

D PREDICT What is the job in the photo? What questions does this person ask?

E PREDICT Match the questions to the answers. Then listen to the conversation to check your answers.

_____ 1. What's your name? a. 1427 Hamilton Street

_____ 2. What's your date of birth? b. Yes, I am.

_____ 3. Why do you want to see the doctor? c. Yasir Abdi

_____ 4. What's your phone number? d. No, I don't.

_____ 5. Where do you live? e. (212) 555-5755

_____ 6. When can you see the doctor? f. I'm tired all the time.

_____ 7. Do you have insurance? g. Monday or Tuesday

_____ 8. Are you a new patient? h. June 28, 1971

F Read. Then answer the questions.

Life ONLINE

> Information about your health is private. Your healthcare provider keeps your information on a secure website. You can log in to the website to access information like your appointments, test results, and medical history. Keep your username and password safe and do not share them with anyone.

1. A secure website is _____.

    a. a website about healthcare   b. a website that is safe

2. Choose the information that is on a secure website.

    a. current medications   b. doctor's office address

G Listen and complete the table.

Name	Symptom(s)	Time and Day	Method of Payment
1. Yasir Abdi			
2. Ming _____			
3. Michael _____			
4. Antonio Marco			
5. Sam _____			

H Choose an illness and complete the table.

Name (What's your name?)	Symptom(s) (What's the matter?)	Time and Day (When can you see the doctor?)	Method of Payment (How will you pay?)

I Use the information from **H** to make a conversation with a partner. Make an appointment to see the doctor.

Receptionist: Hello, Alliance Medical Offices. Can I help you?

Sick Student: Hello, I want to make an appointment to see Dr. Hernandez.

Receptionist: OK. What's your name?

Sick Student: _____

Receptionist: _____

Sick Student: _____

Receptionist: _____

Sick Student: _____

Receptionist: _____

Sick Student: _____

J Perform your conversation for the class.

LESSON 4

Take Two Tablets
GOAL ▶ Read medicine labels

A INTERPRET Underline the words from the box on the medicine label.

aches and pains	exceed	reduce	tablets	uses
directions	persist	symptoms	teenagers	warning

B Match the words with the examples.

_____ 1. Directions   a. for relief of headaches

_____ 2. Uses   b. Don't drive.

_____ 3. Warning   c. Take two tablets.

C DEFINE Match the words with the definitions and examples.

_____ 1. teenager   a. not lasting a long time

_____ 2. temporary   b. continues

_____ 3. do not exceed   c. someone between the ages of 13 and 19

_____ 4. persists   d. no more than

LESSON 4   155

D **Look at the medicines with your classmates and teacher.**

a
cough syrup

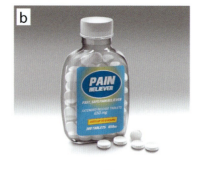
b
pain reliever

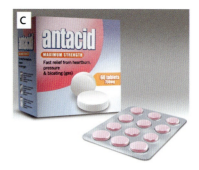
c
antacid

E **IDENTIFY** Read the uses, directions, and warnings for each medicine in **D**. Look up any new words in a dictionary. Then write the correct medicine.

Uses

_____ for temporary relief of headaches or muscle aches and fever

_____ for temporary relief of coughs and throat irritation due to infections

_____ for fast relief of acid indigestion and stomach pain

Directions

_____ Chew 2–4 tablets as needed.

_____ Adults take one or two tablets with water every four hours while symptoms persist. Do not exceed 12 tablets in 24 hours.

_____ Take two teaspoons every four hours.

Warning

_____ Children or teenagers with the flu or chicken pox should NOT take this medicine.

_____ Do not chew more than 12 tablets in 24 hours.

_____ If throat pain persists or coughing is serious, contact your doctor.

Ginger tea can help treat indigestion, sickness, and even stress.

F Study the chart with your classmates and teacher.

Modal: *Should*			
Subject	*Should*	Base Verb	Example Sentence
I	should / shouldn't	take	I **should** take two tablets.
You		chew	You **shouldn't** chew this tablet.
He / She / It		drink	He **shouldn't** drink alcohol with this medicine.
It		hurt	It **shouldn't** hurt.
We / They		swallow	They **should** swallow this tablet with water.

G **PREDICT** Predict which statements are true. Listen to the doctor's instructions. Check (✓) what the patient should do.

1. ☐ He should take medicine and drive.
2. ☐ He should take two pills three times a day.
3. ☐ He should take the pills with water.
4. ☐ He should take three pills two times a day.
5. ☐ He should drink a little alcohol with the medicine.
6. ☐ He should take aspirin and medicine as directed by the doctor.

H Read your answers to **G**. Write statements to describe what you should do with cough syrup. Use the statements for the pain reliever as a model.

Pain reliever:

You should take this medicine for temporary relief of headaches.

You should take one or two tablets every four hours.

Teenagers with chicken pox shouldn't take this medicine.

Cough syrup:

_____

_____

_____

I **APPLY** Find a medicine label at home or online. Share its *uses*, *directions*, and *warnings* with the class.

J Go to the Lifeskills Video Appendix and complete the Unit 6 activities.

LESSON 4

LESSON 5

It's an Emergency!
GOAL ▶ Identify and describe emergencies

A IDENTIFY Look at the emergencies. Label them *medical, police,* and *fire*.

1. _____   2. _____   3. _____

B Read the paragraph and underline the statistics that you see.

Iredell County is located in North Carolina in the United States. It has a website that gives information about the county. According to the website, the county was formed in 1788. It is in the middle of the state and, in 2020, the population was 186,693 people. The website of the sheriff's department also states that, in June 2022, they had 14,428 emergency calls for police assistance, 2,071 calls for fires, and 3,211 medical emergency calls.

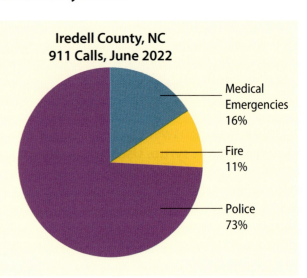

Iredell County, NC
911 Calls, June 2022

- Medical Emergencies 16%
- Fire 11%
- Police 73%

C Answer the questions about the paragraph and pie chart.

1. How many medical emergencies did the county have?
   a. 186,693   b. 16%   c. 3,211

2. How old is the county?
   a. over 200 years old   b. 1788   c. June 2022

3. What percentage of calls were for the police?
   a. 73%   b. 16%   c. 11%

158   UNIT 6

D Listen and practice the conversation.

Operator: 911. What is your emergency?
Teresa: It's a medical emergency.
Operator: What's the problem?
Teresa: My friend is having chest pains.
Operator: I will send an ambulance immediately. What's the address of the emergency?
Teresa: The address is 9976 West Burma Street.
Operator: What's your name and phone number?
Teresa: My name is Teresa, and my cell number is (502) 555-4334. Please hurry!

Simple Past (Irregular)	
Base Verb	Past
break	broke
drink	drank

E Use the emergencies below to practice the conversation in D again.

is unconscious   is choking   drank poison

F **IDENTIFY** Read the emergencies and discuss any new words as a class. Then listen to the conversations and choose the correct answer.

1. a. robbery   b. car accident   c. fire
2. a. heart attack b. fire   c. robbery
3. a. car accident b. robbery   c. fire
4. a. fire   b. robbery   c. heart attack

LESSON 5 159

G SURVEY Read the table with your classmates and teacher. Underline the words you don't know. Complete the table in groups.

	Always call 911.	Never call 911.	Take medicine.	Brand name of medicine
She has a cold.		✓	✓	
A cat is in a tree.				
She has terrible chest pains.				
They have the flu.				
The man is not breathing.				
There is no food in the house.				
I am very tired.				
He coughs every day.				
She has a sore throat.				
She has a stomachache.				
She broke her arm.				
He accidentally drank poison.				

H Practice the conversation. Use the information in **G** to make new conversations.

Student A: What's the matter?
Student B: He accidently drank poison.
Student A: You need to call 911.

Advice	
You should	take call
You need	**to** take **to** call

160   UNIT 6

LESSON 6

Explore the Workforce
GOAL ▶ Explore careers in the medical field

A INTERPRET Work in a group. Look at the graph. What was the most common profession in 2008? How do you know?

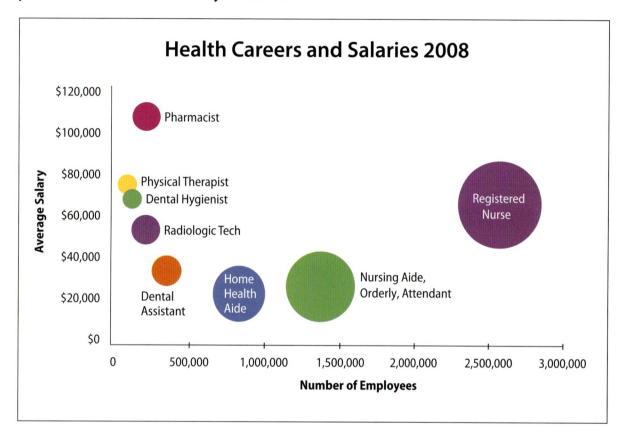

Ask and Answer with *Be* (Past)			
	Subject	***Be***	
Question	What	was	the most common profession in 2008?
Answer	Registered nurse	was	the most common profession.
Question	What	were	the professions with pay between 60k and 80k?

B ANALYZE Use the chart in **A** to answer the questions in full sentences.

1. What was the best paid profession in 2008?

2. What were the two professions with the lowest pay?

3. What were the professions with pay between 60k and 80k?

LESSON 6   161

C Work with a partner. Practice asking and answering the questions in **B** with a partner. Then use the chart in **A** to ask new questions.

D Listen and write the letter of the correct nurse description.

Kind of Nurse	Education You Need	Time It Takes
CNA Certified Nursing Assistant	State-Approved Certificate or Diploma	4 to 12 weeks
LPN Licensed Practical Nurse	State-Approved Certificate or Diploma	12-18 months
RN Registered Nurse	Associate Degree in Nursing (ADN) or Bachelor of Science in Nursing (BSN)	2 years / 4 years
APRN Advanced Practice Registered Nurse	Master of Science in Nursing (MSN) or Doctor of Nursing Practice (DNP)	2 years (post graduate)

1. _____ Takes care of patients and gives medication. Also keeps records and talks to health providers. Helps patients understand their treatment.

2. _____ Works in hospitals and nursing and residential care facilities. A nurse usually gives them jobs to do. Helps patients with daily activities.

3. _____ Can diagnose problems and manage patients. They can order tests and, in some states, they can also prescribe medication.

4. _____ They take vitals and give medication when directed by doctors and RNs.

E **INVESTIGATE** In a group, research online what the salary is for each type of nurse in your state.

CNA: _____

LPN: _____

RN: _____

APRN: _____

F Work in a group. Discuss which kind of nurse you would choose to be.

EXAMPLE: I think LPN is the best for me because I can make a good salary, but I don't have to go to school for very long.

G REFLECT Check what is true about you.

☐ I like to help people.   ☐ I like setting up procedures.

☐ I am warm and caring.   ☐ I make decisions after collecting facts.

☐ I am social.   ☐ I understand what people's needs are.

☐ I am sympathetic.   ☐ I do not like to change my plans.

H INVESTIGATE Work in a group. Follow the steps and research healthcare careers.

1. Go to your favorite search engine.

2. Type "healthcare careers."

3. Open at least three websites.

4. Write five new things you learn.

1. _____

2. _____

3. _____

4. _____

5. _____

I Choose a job title related to healthcare. Go to a job search site online and see if there are any openings within 25 miles of your school or home. Make notes and report to the class.

Student nurses train at a nursing program.

LESSON 6   163

Review

A Look at the photo and write the body parts.

1. _____
2. _____
3. _____
4. _____
5. _____
6. _____
7. _____
8. _____
9. _____
10. _____
11. _____
12. _____
13. _____

B Match each illness to the advice.

_____ 1. I have a headache.
_____ 2. I have a bad toothache.
_____ 3. I have a stomachache.
_____ 4. I have chest pains.

a. You should go to the dentist.
b. You should call 911 right now.
c. You should take a pain reliever.
d. You should chew some antacid tablets.

Learner Log I can identify illnesses.
☐ Yes ☐ No ☐ Maybe

C Give someone advice on how to stay healthy. Write two things the person should do and two things he or she shouldn't do. Use the photos to help you.

should do

a. _____

b. _____

shouldn't do

a. _____

b. _____

D Complete the sentences with the simple past form of the verbs in parentheses.

1. Yesterday, I _____ (have) a terrible headache.

2. Suzanne _____ (be) sick last week.

3. Last summer, we _____ (talk) to the doctor.

4. I _____ (go) to the hospital on Monday.

5. They _____ (call) the doctor five minutes ago.

6. Last year, the children _____ (be) sick a lot.

7. The doctor _____ (say) I shouldn't smoke.

8. He _____ (go) to the doctor's last week.

E Match the section of the medicine label to the information.

1. _____ Uses   a. Take two tablets three times a day.

2. _____ Directions   b. Do not take more than 12 tablets in 24 hours.

3. _____ Warning   c. for the temporary relief of aches and pains

Learner Log I can describe healthy practices.   I can make a doctor's appointment.
☐ Yes ☐ No ☐ Maybe   ☐ Yes ☐ No ☐ Maybe

Review

F Put the conversation in the correct order.

_____ Mario: 66345 West Malvern Avenue.

_____ Operator: Is anyone injured?

_____ Mario: There is a fire!

__1__ Operator: 911. What's your emergency?

_____ Operator: A fire? What's your name?

_____ Mario: I don't think so. Please hurry.

_____ Mario: Thank you!

_____ Operator: Yes, sir. They will be there very soon.

_____ Operator: Yes, of course. What is the address?

_____ Mario: Mario de la Vega. Please send the fire department.

G Write the symptom under each picture and a possible medicine.

1.

Symptom: _____

Medicine: _____

2.

Symptom: _____

Medicine: _____

3.

Symptom: _____

Medicine: _____

4.

Symptom: _____

Medicine: _____

| **Learner Log** | I can read medicine labels.
☐ Yes ☐ No ☐ Maybe | I can identify and describe emergencies.
☐ Yes ☐ No ☐ Maybe |

Team Project

Make a Health Pamphlet
SOFT SKILL ▶ Active Listening

In a group, you are going to design a health pamphlet for the community. The pamphlet will give health tips and explain what medicines to take for common illnesses.

1. Form a team with four or five students. In your team, you need:

Position	Job Description	Student Name
Student 1: **Team Leader**	Check that everyone speaks English. Check that everyone participates.	
Student 2: **Nurse**	Give advice on medicines for three illnesses.	
Student 3: **Health Expert**	Give advice on three things to do to stay healthy.	
Students 4/5: **Artists**	Design pamphlet and prepare a class presentation with help from the team.	

2. Health Expert, tell your team three things people should do to be healthy and three things people should not do.

3. Think of three common illnesses to include in your pamphlet and describe them.

4. Nurse, tell your team about medicines people should take for these illnesses.

   Compliment: "That's a great medicine for a cough."

   Improvement: "I don't think that medicine is the best choice for a headache. Let's think about a different choice."

5. Artists, collect and organize the information to design a pamphlet with pictures.

6. Choose a student to present the information and practice the presentation.

ACTIVE LISTENING:
Giving Feedback
Feedback is not only about how something can improve. It is also about complimenting others on their ideas.

Reading Challenge

A Work in a group. Put the activities in order from least dangerous (1) to most dangerous (7).

_____ exercising

_____ skiing

_____ rock climbing with ropes

_____ rock climbing with no ropes

_____ driving a car

_____ flying in a plane

__1__ watching TV

B Read the title and skim the text. What is the dangerous passion?

C Read. Underline any words you don't know.

D What is another good title for the text?

  1. A Terrible Accident

  2. A Long Recovery

  3. An Unsafe Mountain

  4. A Risky Hobby

E In line 3, *a little equipment* means _____.

  1. equipment that is small in size
  2. not much equipment
  3. equipment for ropes
  4. filming equipment

F According to the text, who do you call in an emergency on a mountain?

  1. doctors
  2. friends
  3. ski patrol
  4. Jackson

G Do you have a passion? Tell a partner.

A Dangerous Passion

Renan Ozturk is a Turkish-American rock climber and photographer. His mother is American, and his father is Turkish. He has climbed some of the world's most dangerous mountains. He often climbs with no ropes and only a little equipment.* Renan likes to film his climbs and share his experiences with people. When he is climbing, Renan says to himself, "No mistakes," because just one mistake means he could fall.

In 2011, Renan had a terrible accident in Jackson, Wyoming, but he wasn't climbing. He was skiing with friends and fell 1,000 feet. His friends called the Jackson Ski Patrol, who rushed Renan to a medical center. He broke bones in his neck, and he had a serious head injury. He needed to wear a neck brace* for three months.

Renan almost died, but he loves being outdoors and he loves climbing. Five months after the accident, Renan was climbing again, and in 2019, he climbed the highest mountain in the world.

equipment things you use to do something
brace something somebody wears to support a part of the body

Renan looks out from his tent on the side of a mountain.

7 Work, Work, Work

UNIT OUTCOMES

▸ Evaluate learning and work skills
▸ Identify jobs and job skills
▸ Apply for a job
▸ Interview for a job
▸ Follow instructions in an office
▸ Compare and contrast jobs in business administration

Look at the photo and answer the questions.

1. Where are the women in the photo?
2. What is the machine in this photo?

Two women work on an assembly line at the General Motors Flint Assembly Plant in Flint, Michigan.

1. What is an assembly line?
2. Do you think the two women in the photo have a difficult job? Why?

171

LESSON 1
A Good Student and Employee
GOAL ▶ Evaluate learning and work skills

A LIST What characteristics do a good student and a good employee have?

Student	Employee

B Read about Dasma and good work habits. Underline any new words. 🎧

Dasma is an English student in Dearborn, Michigan. She needs a job. She had several jobs before she started studying. She was a cashier and an administrative assistant. She's a good worker and a good student. She comes to school on time every day, participates, and has a positive attitude. She helps other students and they help her.

Good work habits are very important in the United States. Employees who come on time, work hard, and cooperate are more successful than other employees. Good work habits in the classroom are similar to good work habits in the workplace.

C EVALUATE Are you a good student with good work habits? Circle the number that best describes you.

	Never			Always
1. I come to class every day.	1	2	3	4
2. I come to class on time.	1	2	3	4
3. I participate in class and in groups.	1	2	3	4
4. I do my homework.	1	2	3	4
5. I listen carefully.	1	2	3	4
6. I help others.	1	2	3	4

D INTERPRET Look at Dasma's employee evaluation form from 2023.

Fairview Hotel Employee Performance Review			
Name: Dasma Shir **Supervisor:** Patricia Bastos **Position:** Administrative Assistant **Date:** January 4th, 2023			
EVALUATION			
	E = Exceeds Expectations	G = Good	NI = Needs Improvement
1. Attendance	☐	☐	☐
2. Quality of Work	☐	☐	☐
3. Commitment	☐	☐	☐
4. Relations with Others	☐	☐	☐
5. Job Knowledge	☐	☐	☐
Dasma is a new employee. She still has more to learn.			
6. Attitude	☐	☐	☐
Dasma enjoys her job and is always cheerful.			

Supervisor's signature: _____

Employee's signature: _____

E Listen to the conversation between Dasma and her boss about her evaluation. Check the correct information (*E*, *G*, or *NI*) on the form. 🎧

F RANK In a group, talk about which characteristics are the most important to have at work. Number the characteristics from 1 to 6. *1* is the most important characteristic.

_____ Comes to work on time

_____ Does quality work

_____ Is committed to the company

_____ Works well with others

_____ Understands the job

_____ Has a positive attitude

LESSON 1 173

G Study the charts with your classmates and teacher.

Future: *Will* (Affirmative)			
Subject	Will	Base Verb	Example Sentence
I		come	I **will come** to class on time.
You		listen	You **will listen** carefully and follow directions.
He		work	He **will work** hard.
She	will	understand	She **will understand** the job.
It		help	It **will help**.
We		have	We **will have** a positive attitude.
They		do	They **will do** their homework.

Future: *Will* (Negative)			
Subject	Will	Base Verb	Example Sentence
I / You		come	I **won't come** to class late.
He / She	will not (won't)	leave	He **won't leave** class early.
It		help	It **won't help**.
We / They		forget	We **will not forget** our homework.

H Complete the sentences with the future form of the verbs in parentheses. Use the affirmative for things that are good to do at school. Use the negative for things that are bad to do at school.

1. I _____*will come*_____ (come) to school on time every day.

2. Barry _____ (smoke) in class.

3. We _____ (participate) in groups.

4. You _____ (have) a positive attitude.

5. They _____ (forget) their notebooks.

6. I _____ (listen) carefully.

I **PLAN** Work with a partner. Talk about two things you plan to do at school. In your notebook, write your ideas and your partner's ideas using the future.

174 UNIT 7

LESSON 2

What Can You Do?

GOAL ▶ Identify jobs and job skills

A   IDENTIFY Write each job title under the correct picture.

| administrative assistant | home health aide | hotel clerk | musician |
| construction worker | homemaker | landscaper | retail salesperson |

Kim
1. _____

Chang
2. _____

Ivan
3. _____

Diwa
4. _____

Imani
5. _____

Avi
6. _____

Claire
7. _____

Keegan
8. _____

B   Practice the conversation. Make new conversations using the information in A.

Student A: What does Claire do?

Student B: She's an administrative assistant.

C Work with a partner. Look at the tools and instruments. Discuss what they are used for.

blood pressure monitor   wrench   wheelbarrow   computer

D **CLASSIFY** Look at the jobs and write one or two tools or instruments for each job. Then complete the skills using the words in the box.

builds houses	helps students	repairs machinery	writes emails
checks blood pressure	listens carefully	trims trees	writes programs
checks people in	prepares meals		

Job	Tool or Instrument	Skill
administrative assistant		
computer programmer		
construction worker		
cook		
hotel clerk		
landscaper		
mechanic		
nurse		
student		
teacher		

E **INTERPRET** Dasma is interviewing for a job. Read the skills and work history sections of her job application. Then listen and write the dates and job responsibilities.

SKILLS
Skills: comfortable with office computer programs and applications, strong in customer service
Languages: French, Arabic (fluent), and English (beginner)

WORK HISTORY				
Position	**Company**	**From**	**To**	**Responsibilities**
Administrative Assistant	Fairview Hotel			

Reason for Leaving
I left to attend school.

Position	**Company**	**From**	**To**	**Responsibilities**
Cashier	Al Ameer Restaurant			

Reason for Leaving
I moved.

Can	*Can't*
I **can** type.	I **can't** type.
He **can** type.	He **can't** type.

F According to Dasma's job application in E, what can she do? Write sentences about her skills.

1. She _____
2. _____
3. _____
4. _____

G Work with a partner. What can you do? What can your partner do?

You

_____
_____
_____

Your partner

_____
_____
_____

LESSON 2

LESSON 3

Job Hunting

GOAL ▶ Apply for a job

A INTERPRET Scan the job posts. Complete the table.

APARTMENT MANAGER
Full-time position for a bilingual (Spanish and English) apartment manager.
Must have two years' experience in painting and doing minor maintenance.

FULL-TIME COOK
Full-time cook position at Martha's Kitchen.
No experience required as training will be given.
Flexible hours.

CASHIER
Part-time cashier position at Franklin's Cinema.
$11.00 per hour.
No experience necessary.

DRIVER
Full-time driver position for Alexander's Furniture Warehouse.
$16.75 per hour.
Commercial driver's license required.
Monday–Friday, 6:00 a.m.–2:30 p.m.

LEGAL ASSISTANT
Full-time position for a bilingual (Farsi and English) legal assistant at Smith and Khan Law Offices.
Good organizational skills required.
Available immediately.

ESL TEACHER
Part-time position for an ESL teacher at Casper Education Center.
BA and one year's teaching experience required.
Benefits available.

BA
A **B**achelor of **A**rts degree is a degree from a university.

Information	Jobs
full-time	
part-time	
paid hourly	
needs a BA degree	
needs a driver's license	
needs no experience	

178   UNIT 7

B Ask and answer questions with a partner about the information in the ads in **A**.

EXAMPLE:

1. Is the apartment manager job full-time or part-time?

2. How much experience do you need for the apartment manager job?

3. How many languages do you need to speak for the apartment manager job?

C **COLLABORATE** Read about the people with your classmates and teacher. Practice pronunciation by emphasizing the words and syllables in bold. Then, with a partner, decide which job in **A** is best for each person.

Stress
Place stress on words or syllables that are important in a sentence:
Who is a hard worker?
SILvia is a hard worker.
What kind of worker is Silvia?
Silvia is a **HARD** worker.

1. **Sil**via is a **hard** worker. She can work **full**-time or **part**-time. She speaks **Eng**lish well. She can work in an **office** and is very organized.

Job: _____

2. **Tanh** is always on time for **work**. He has a **driv**er's license and knows how to drive a **truck**.

Job: _____

3. **Let**i has **three** children and wants to stay home with them, but she needs to **work**. She can **fix** things around the house. Her **rent** is **very** expensive.

Job: _____

4. **Ri**go needs a **full**-time po**sit**ion. He doesn't have any ex**per**ience. He wants to learn something **new**.

Job: _____

D Listen to Gloria and Esteban talk about some of the job posts in **A**. Write the titles of the jobs they are talking about.

1. _____

2. _____

3. _____

4. _____

LESSON 3   179

E APPLY Complete the application for yourself.

APPLICATION FOR EMPLOYMENT

PERSONAL INFORMATION

Name: _____ Date: _____

Address: _____

Social security number: _____ Phone: _____

Position applied for: _____

SKILLS

Skills: _____

Languages: _____

WORK HISTORY

Position	Company	From	To	Responsibilities

Reason for Leaving

Position	Company	From	To	Responsibilities

Reason for Leaving

F Read some Dos and Don'ts of applying for a job online. Look up any new words in a dictionary.

Do…
- study the job post to learn what the company is looking for.
- prepare a resume that matches the position. Use keywords in your resume.
- check that the site is real, not fake. Research the company before you apply.
- review your application before sending it. Answer all the questions.
- make sure to send your application through a secure website with a login.

Don't…
- lie in your application.
- apply if you think the company may be fake.
- pay to apply for a job.
- email your social security number.

Be very careful with your social security number. Scammers can use it to steal your identity. Legally, you don't have to give your number until you get the job, but some employers want it so they can do background checks. Politely ask why they need the number if you are worried about it.

G Search online for "job search websites" for your area. Write three URLs in your notebook.

LESSON 4

Job Interviews
GOAL ▶ Interview for a job

A Dasma is interviewing for another job. Look again at her work history.

WORK HISTORY				
Position	**Company**	**From**	**To**	**Responsibilities**
Administrative Assistant	Fairview Hotel	December 2019	November 2022	
Reason for Leaving I left to attend school.				
Position	**Company**	**From**	**To**	**Responsibilities**
Cashier	Al Ameer Restaurant	June 2016	November 2019	
Reason for Leaving I moved.				

B Listen to the conversation and choose *True* or *False*.

1. Dasma was a cashier at Al Ameer Restaurant.   True   False
2. Dasma was a desk clerk at the Fairview Hotel.   True   False
3. Dasma answered the phone at the Fairview Hotel.   True   False
4. Dasma talked to guests at the Fairview Hotel.   True   False

C Read and listen to the conversation. Check your answers to B.

Ms. Cardoza: Good afternoon, Ms. Shir. Please sit down. I have your application here. You were a desk clerk at the Fairview Hotel and before that you were a cashier. Is that right?

Dasma: I was an administrative assistant at the Fairview Hotel. I wasn't a desk clerk.

Ms. Cardoza: Oh, yes, that's right. What kind of work did you do?

Dasma: I checked reservations and wrote emails.

Ms. Cardoza: So, you didn't answer the phone or talk to guests?

Dasma: No, I didn't talk to guests, but I learn quickly and speak many languages.

Ms. Cardoza: Did you work in the evenings?

Dasma: No, I didn't work in the evenings. I finished at 6:30 p.m.

Ms. Cardoza: Thank you, Ms. Shir. We will call you.

D Read about job interviews. Look up any new words in the dictionary.

The job interview is an important step in getting a job. Yes, the application is important—a well-presented application can help you get an interview, but a bad interview means no job! **Interviewers** look for many things in an interview. **Among other things**, the **employer** wants an **employee** who has a positive attitude and is confident.
5 The employer knows that a worker with a good attitude will probably work hard and stay on the job.

The **prospective** employee will show confidence in many ways in the interview. For example, he or she will look the employer in the eye and give a **firm** handshake. He or she will speak confidently and listen carefully to the questions. The **interviewee** will also
10 dress nicely and be prepared for the interview by doing research about the company and the position. All of these things—**along with** not smoking, eating, or chewing gum—will ensure a good interview.

E **SOLVE** Match the new words with the definitions or examples.

_____ 1. along with   a. company; boss; supervisor

_____ 2. among other things b. including

_____ 3. employee   c. possible in the future

_____ 4. employer   d. strong

_____ 5. firm   e. the person giving the interview

_____ 6. interviewee   f. the person in the interview who is looking for a job

_____ 7. interviewer   g. There are many things. This is one of them.

_____ 8. prospective   h. worker

F Some interviews are online. Read the list. With a group. Write a check (✓) next to the things you should do in an online interview, and write X next to what you should not do.

Life ONLINE

be casual during _____   keep a messy desk _____
choose a busy place before _____ look into the camera during _____
prepare your materials before _____ answer your phone during _____
come a few minutes early _____   test the technology before _____

G Study the charts with your classmates and teacher.

Simple Past (Regular)	
Subject	**Past Verb (Base + -ed)**
I / He / She / It We / You / They	checked. worked. cooked.

Simple Past: *Be*	
Subject	***Be***
I / He / She / It	was.
We / You / They	were.

Negative Simple Past (Regular)		
Subject	***Did* + *not***	**Base Verb**
I / He / She / It We / You / They	did not (didn't)	check. work. cook.

Negative Simple Past: *Be*	
Subject	***Be* + *not***
I / He / She / It	was not (wasn't).
We / You / They	were not (weren't).

H Refer to **A** and answer the questions using the negative simple past.

1. Was Dasma a student in 2022?

   Dasma _____*wasn't*_____ a student in 2022. She was a student in 2023.

2. Did Dasma move in 2015?

   Dasma _____ in 2015. She moved in 2019.

3. Did Dasma work at the Fairmont Hotel?

   Dasma _____ at the Fairmont Hotel. She worked at the Fairview Hotel.

4. Did Dasma and Ms. Cardoza talk about the weather?

   Dasma and Ms. Cardoza _____ about the weather. They talked about Dasma's work experience.

5. Were Dasma and Ms. Cardoza at a restaurant?

   Dasma and Ms. Cardoza _____ at a restaurant. They were in an office.

6. Was Dasma late for the job interview?

   Dasma _____ late for the interview. She was on time.

I **CREATE** Work with a partner. Write a conversation that is a job interview. Share it with the class.

LESSON 5

How Does It Work?

GOAL ▶ Follow instructions in an office

A IDENTIFY Write the correct letter next to each object in the picture.

| a. badge | b. badge reader | c. laptop | d. plug | e. printer/copier |

B SEQUENCE Listen to the instructions for the copier. Number the instructions in the correct order. 🎧

_____ Choose the number of copies.

_____ Place the original on the glass.

___1___ Open the lid.

_____ Press the Start button.

_____ Close the lid.

C Write the names of the objects.

1. _____ 2. _____ 3. _____

D Use the words from the box to complete the directions. Then write the task that you want to complete. You may use some of the words more than once.

| choose | close | enter | open | put | wait |
| click | connect | follow | press | select | |

1. **Task:** _____
   _____ the document on your computer.
   _____ File > Print.
   _____ the number of copies.
   _____ the Print button.

2. **Task:** _____
   _____ your badge in front of the badge reader.
   _____ for the light to turn green.
   _____ the door.
   _____ the office.

3. **Task:** _____
   _____ the machine to a computer or a network.
   _____ the lid.
   _____ the item face down on the screen.
   _____ the lid.
   _____ Start.
   _____ the instructions on your computer screen.

E Study the chart with your classmates and teacher.

Imperatives		
	Base Verb	**Example Sentence**
~~you~~	open follow print	Open the document. Follow the instructions on your computer screen. Print your document.

F We use imperatives to give instructions. Write the instructions for the objects in **C**. Start each sentence with a verb.

Projector Instructions

<u>Turn on the projector. Plug the video cable into the computer. Open your document.</u>

<u>Share your screen.</u>

Copier Instructions

_____

_____

Tablet Instructions

_____

_____

G **APPLY** Work in a group. Think of another machine (microwave, washing machine, vending machine, etc.) and write instructions. Look for ideas online.

_____

_____

_____

_____

_____

_____

LESSON 6: Explore the Workforce

GOAL ▶ Compare and contrast jobs in business administration

A **INTERPRET** Look at the infographic and answer the questions.

1. What education do you need for an administrative assistant position?

2. How much more is the average salary for Tier IV than Tier III?

3. What are the three positions that pay between $30,000 and $40,000?

4. What positions don't require a Bachelor's degree?

BUSINESS ADMINISTRATION CAREERS

TIER IV	AVERAGE SALARY: $113,220
Purchasing Manager — BACHELOR'S DEGREE — $127,150	Administrative Services Manager — BACHELOR'S DEGREE — $99,290

TIER III	AVERAGE SALARY: $73,440
Training Development Specialist — BACHELOR'S DEGREE — $61,570	Business Operations Specialist — BACHELOR'S DEGREE — $85,310

TIER II	AVERAGE SALARY: $56,810
Office Supervisor & Administrative Worker — BACHELOR'S DEGREE — $63,380	Human Resources Specialist — BACHELOR'S DEGREE — $62,290	Payroll Clerk — SOME COLLEGE, NO DEGREE — $44,760

TIER I	AVERAGE SALARY: $38,215
Human Resources Assistant — ASSOCIATE'S DEGREE — $37,600	Financial Clerk — HIGH SCHOOL DIPLOMA — $38,830

BASELINE POSITION
Administrative Assistant — HIGH SCHOOL DIPLOMA — $39,680

B Match the job title with the description.

_____ 1. Payroll Clerk

_____ 2. Purchasing Manager

_____ 3. Human Resources Specialist

_____ 4. Financial Clerk

_____ 5. Training Development Specialist

a. manages employees who buy products for the company or organization

b. develops training for employees

c. manages the payment of wages to employees

d. helps find and hire new employees

e. handles money and helps customers with financial transactions

C Ask a partner what workers do in different positions.

Example:

Student 1: *What does an office supervisor do?*

Student 2: *An office supervisor makes sure all office work is done on time and also does many tasks in the office, like filing and producing reports.*

D Look at the graphic. What parts of the administrative assistant position do you think are most difficult for you? Circle them in the picture.

E Work with a group. Rank the job duties from easiest (1) to most difficult (6).

_____ send emails

_____ write reports

_____ use software programs

_____ design and maintain filing system

_____ maintain financial information

_____ communicate effectively with employees and administrators

F Read about English skills needed to be an effective administrative assistant. Where can you go to improve your writing skills?

> Administrative assistants need good skills in writing standard English. They can learn these skills in English as a Second Language classes, standard English classes, and business writing courses at community colleges, adult schools, private language schools, vocational business schools, or through e-learning. If you pay close attention to detail and work hard, you can achieve your goals. If you have good writing skills, the quality of your work will improve your chances of getting a job.

G Work with a partner. Talk about what you learned about an administrative assistant position. Do you think you can do the work?

H **REFLECT** Check what is true about you.

☐ I am friendly. ☐ I follow instructions well.

☐ I am good at organizing. ☐ I like solving problems.

☐ I like working closely with others. ☐ I am detail-oriented.

☐ I manage my time well. ☐ I am helpful.

I **INVESTIGATE** Work in a group. Follow the steps and research office careers.

1. Go to your favorite search engine.

2. Type "office careers."

3. Open at least three websites.

4. Write five new things you learn.

1. _____

2. _____

3. _____

4. _____

5. _____

J Choose a job title related to office work. Do a job search online and see if there are any openings within 25 miles of your school or home. What are three duties of the position according to the job post? Write them in your notebook.

Review

A Look at the two sections from Youssouf's job application.

SKILLS				
Technical Skills: Advanced programming; knowledge of many software programs				
Languages: French (bilingual)				
WORK HISTORY				
Position	Company	From	To	Responsibilities
Computer Programmer	Datamix Computers	June, 2021	Present	
Reason for Leaving				
Position	Company	From	To	Responsibilities
Assembly Worker	Datamix Computers	April, 2017	May, 2021	
Reason for Leaving Promotion				

B Look at the skills section. Write sentences about what Youssouf can and can't do.

1. speak French   _Youssouf can speak French._
2. speak Spanish _____
3. build a house _____
4. use software programs _____

C Look at Youssouf's job history. Complete the sentences with the correct negative or affirmative form of the verb in parentheses.

1. Youssouf _____ (work) at Datamix Computers in 2016.
2. Youssouf _____ (be) an assembly worker at Datamix Computers in 2018.
3. Youssouf _____ (start) his first job at Datamix in April, 2017.
4. Youssouf _____ (be) a programmer from April, 2017 to May, 2021.
5. Youssouf _____ (change) his job in April, 2021.

Learner Log   I can interview for a job.
☐ Yes   ☐ No   ☐ Maybe

D Write the name of the objects.

1. _____ 2. _____ 3. _____

E Match the correct verb with the instruction.

_____ 1. Press   a. the paper in the machine.

_____ 2. Place   b. the instructions.

_____ 3. Follow   c. Start.

F Complete the sentences about school with the future (*will*) affirmative or negative.

1. I _____*will come*_____ (come) to work on time every day.

2. We _____ (eat) in class.

3. They _____ (play) basketball in class.

4. I _____ (work) with a partner.

5. You _____ (do) the homework every day.

6. They _____ (have) a good attitude.

7. She _____ (sleep) in class.

8. Dasma _____ (like) this class.

Learner Log

I can follow instructions in an office.
☐ Yes ☐ No ☐ Maybe

I can evaluate learning and work skills.
☐ Yes ☐ No ☐ Maybe

Review

G Write the name of the job under the picture.

1. _____

2. _____

3. _____

4. _____

5. _____

6. _____

H Read the job posts. Complete the table below.

HELP WANTED
Full-time facilities manager at John Adams School.
No experience needed.
$17 an hour.
Benefits included.

HELP WANTED
Part-time mechanic.
One year's experience required.
$20.00 per hour.

HELP WANTED
Full-time nurse position at Mayfield Hospital Tuesday through Saturday.
AA degree and one year's experience required.

Position	Pay	Experience	Part-time/Full-time
1.			
2.			
3.			

Learner Log

I can identify jobs and job skills.
☐ Yes ☐ No ☐ Maybe

I can apply for a job.
☐ Yes ☐ No ☐ Maybe

Team Project

Make Your Own Company
SOFT SKILL ▶ ACTIVE LISTENING

In a group, you are going to make a new company. Write job advertisements and interview new employees.

1. Form a team of four or five students. In your team, you need:

Position	Job Description	Student Name
Student 1: **Team Leader**	Check that everyone speaks English. Check that everyone participates.	
Student 2: **Recruiter**	Write a classified ad with help from the team.	
Student 3: **Designer**	Prepare an application form with help from the team.	
Students 4/5: **Interviewers**	Prepare interview questions with help from the team.	

2. You are the owners of a new company. What is the name of your company? What kind of company is it?

3. What job are you going to advertise? What information will you put in the advertisement?

4. What questions will you have on the application form? What questions will you ask at the job interview?

5. Interview four students for your job.

6. Decide who you will hire and present your work to the class.

ACTIVE LISTENING
Asking for Clarification

When sharing ideas, it is important that you understand all the ideas clearly. One way to do that is to ask for clarification. Here are some ways to ask for clarification.

Could you say that again, please?
What do you mean exactly?
If I understand correctly, you mean…
I'm sorry, I didn't hear you.

It is also very important that you show respect for the person speaking with your body language by nodding, making eye contact, and not looking down at your phone or around the room.

Reading Challenge

A Work with a partner. Answer the questions.

1. Do you have a career now?
2. Do you want a career?
3. If you want a career, how hard do you want to work for it?
4. What level of English do you need to be successful in your career?

B Read. Underline any words you don't know.

C Based on the reading, what do you think these words mean?

1. perspectives (line 1)
   - a. points of view
   - b. people
   - c. situations

2. passion (line 2)
   - a. something you like
   - b. a hobby
   - c. something you're very excited about

3. joy (line 2)
   - a. happiness
   - b. sadness
   - c. anger

4. mentor (line 11)
   - a. a close friend
   - b. an experienced advisor
   - c. a teacher

D Choose the best answer.

1. When Eli left Chile, she wanted to _____
   - a. be a teacher.
   - b. work in a bank in Chile.
   - c. make new friends and find mentors.
   - d. help other immigrants.

2. Eli studied English in Santa Ana because _____
   - a. she wanted to find good teachers.
   - b. they had good finance classes.
   - c. she learned quickly.
   - d. she didn't have to pay.

E Tell a partner Eli's story in your own words.

F What steps do you need to take to start a career or achieve other things that you want in life? Write the steps.

Hard Work or Passion?

With every experience come new **perspectives** that can shape futures. Finding your **passion** and working hard can lead to success and **joy**. This is true for Elizabeth Dinamarca Clarke.

Eli traveled to the United States in 2001 from her native country of Chile. She wanted to learn English and then return to her country to work at a bank or in finances. She looked for a program that was not too expensive in Southern California. She found a free program at Santa Ana College.

Her first experiences in school changed her view on life. She studied hard both day and night and learned what she called "this crazy language." She also started tutoring others and teaching computer classes at the school while she studied English. She saw the passion of several teachers who today are her **mentors** and friends. These role models helped her develop a love for English, and her feelings about the future changed. She found her passion! She decided to learn English quickly and well so she could one day help other immigrants.

It wasn't easy, and it took a lot of dedication, but Eli completed a master's degree program in San Diego. Now she has a full-time teaching position at MiraCosta College. Eli teaches English and computer classes to immigrants who want to learn the language. There is no doubt that she teaches with the same passion and love for her students that she experienced more than 20 years earlier.

Elizabeth Dinamarca Clarke

"I enjoy helping our students achieve their dreams of learning the language to improve their lives, to communicate in their communities, to further their education, or to simply help their children with homework. Impacting students' lives through teaching is my passion!"

8 Goals and Lifelong Learning

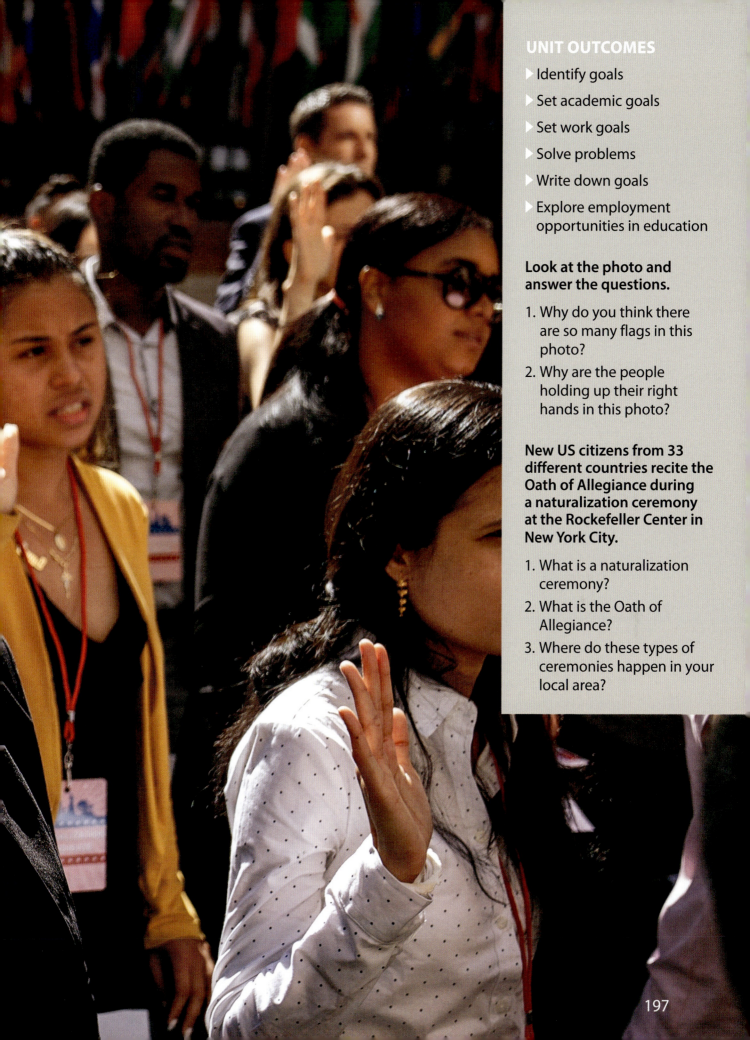

UNIT OUTCOMES

- Identify goals
- Set academic goals
- Set work goals
- Solve problems
- Write down goals
- Explore employment opportunities in education

Look at the photo and answer the questions.

1. Why do you think there are so many flags in this photo?
2. Why are the people holding up their right hands in this photo?

New US citizens from 33 different countries recite the Oath of Allegiance during a naturalization ceremony at the Rockefeller Center in New York City.

1. What is a naturalization ceremony?
2. What is the Oath of Allegiance?
3. Where do these types of ceremonies happen in your local area?

LESSON 1

What Is Success?
GOAL ▶ Identify goals

A Read and discuss.

> What is success? One dictionary defines success as "getting something you want." Some people think that means a good job and a lot of money. Other people think that means a healthy life, love, and family. What does success mean for you?

B **RANK** What is most important to you? Number the items from 1 to 6. 1 is the most important to you.

_____ family

_____ money

_____ entertainment

_____ employment

_____ friends

_____ education

C Read about Kossi's goals.

> Kossi is from Togo. Togo is a country in West Africa. Kossi's career is important to him. He wants to be a pediatrician one day. He loves kids and likes to help people. He is studying English and wants to get an Associate degree in science first. Then he plans to go to a university. He is working in a restaurant and also as an administrative assistant to make money so he can go to school. Kossi knows that he will need to work very hard to be successful and reach his goals.

D Work in a group. Talk about the questions.

1. What is Kossi's career goal?

2. Why do you think he wants to be a pediatrician?

3. Why do you think he has more than one job now?

E Read about goal setting. Discuss goals you have with the class.

> Goal setting is important because it helps people think about their future and work toward it. If we don't have goals, it may take us longer to get what we want in life. It is important to set goals that are difficult, but goals that we can really reach. For best success, we should review our goals often and we should write them down.

F Listen to Carmen's goals and check the goals that you hear.

- ☐ buy a house
- ☐ keep a job
- ☐ participate in her child's school
- ☐ get married
- ☐ learn new skills at work
- ☐ get a high school diploma
- ☐ have children
- ☐ get a promotion
- ☐ go to college
- ☐ become a citizen
- ☐ get a better job
- ☐ graduate from college
- ☐ get a job
- ☑ study English

G **CLASSIFY** Look at Carmen's goals in **F**. Write them in the correct boxes.

Personal and Family

Vocational (work)

Academic (educational)
She wants to study English.

LESSON 1 199

H Study the charts with your classmates and teacher.

Future Plans: *Want to, Hope to, Plan to*		
Subject	Verb	Infinitive (*to* + Base)
I / You / We / They	hope, want, plan	to study in school for three years. to graduate from college. to get married.
He / She / It	hopes, wants, plans	

Future Plans: *Be Going to*		
Subject	*Be Going to*	Base Verb
I	am going to	get a high school diploma.
You / We / They	are going to	participate in class.
He / She / It	is going to	buy a house.

	want to	hope to	plan to	be going to	
less definite	←			→	more definite

I Complete the sentences expressing future plans with the correct form of the verbs.

1. Carmen and Marie _____*want to speak*_____ (want / speak) English.

2. I _____ (plan / come) to class on time every day.

3. Marie _____ (hope / be) a nurse someday.

4. Lien _____ (be going to / graduate) from college.

5. Marco and I _____ (plan / visit) Mexico in the future.

6. They _____ (want / move), but they have a three-year lease.

J **PLAN** Write two of your future plans. Then ask a partner about their future plans.

My future plans

_____

_____

My partner's future plans

_____

_____

LESSON 2: Education in the United States

GOAL ▶ Set academic goals

A **INTERPRET** Discuss the pie chart with your classmates and teacher.

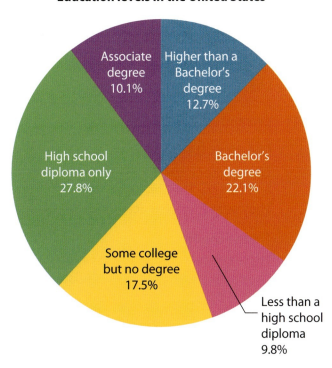

Education levels in the United States

- Associate degree 10.1%
- Higher than a Bachelor's degree 12.7%
- Bachelor's degree 22.1%
- Less than a high school diploma 9.8%
- Some college but no degree 17.5%
- High school diploma only 27.8%

B Practice the conversation. Make new conversations using the information in the pie chart.

Student A: What percentage of people in the United States has less than a high school diploma?
Student B: 9.8%

C **PLAN** Write one academic goal that you have. Use the grammar in Lesson 1 to express future plans.

_____

_____

D Listen to the lecture. Write down two or more diplomas, certificates, or degrees you hear.

_____

_____

E Read and discuss the educational choices adults have in the United States.

High School Diploma
Some adult schools have high school classes where you can earn a high school diploma.

Certificates
Certificates for specific trades like nursing, computer programming, and mechanics can be earned from trade schools, some junior colleges, and some adult schools.

BA / BS Degree
These are called Bachelor of Arts or Bachelor of Science degrees. Adults earn these degrees from a four-year college or university.

GED
Some adult schools have classes to help you prepare for a test. If you pass the test, you earn a GED, or General Equivalency Diploma. This diploma is similar to a high school diploma.

AA / AS Degree
This is called an Associate of Arts or an Associate of Science degree. Adults earn this degree from a two-year junior or community college.

Graduate Degree
After earning a Bachelor's degree, adults can study more and receive additional degrees.

Adult Schools
These schools are sometimes free. Students learn basic skills like reading and writing. They can learn about jobs and computers. These schools can help students get their GED and some certificates.

Junior Colleges / Community Colleges
These schools are not expensive for residents. They offer two-year academic, technical, and vocational courses. They help students prepare for universities or jobs. Students can study part time in the evenings or on the weekends.

Colleges / Universities
These schools prepare students for jobs and careers. They are often very expensive. They offer four-year academic courses.

Trade Schools
These schools are sometimes expensive. They help students learn job-related skills, such as computers or mechanics.

F Read again. Match the questions to the answers.

__b__ 1. Why is it good to get a high school diploma?

_____ 2. Why do people go to a two-year college?

_____ 3. Why do people go to a university?

_____ 4. Why do people go to an adult school?

a. to learn how to read and write English or to get a GED

b. to get a better job or prepare to go to a two-year college or university

c. to get an Associate degree, to get a better job, or to prepare to go to a university

d. to qualify for a career or to get a Bachelor's degree

G Students can earn some degrees online. Look at the table of advantages and disadvantages. Search online for "advantages and disadvantages of online courses." Complete the table.

Advantages	Disadvantages
flexible schedule	less collaboration with other students

H Study the chart with your classmates and teacher.

Statement	Because		
	Because	Subject + Verb	Information
Marie plans to go to college	because	she wants	to be a nurse.
Lien hopes to learn English		she plans	to go to college.
They hope to go to an adult school		they want	to learn English.
I want to go to a trade school		I want	to be a mechanic.

I **PLAN** Read the example and write your own story.

> Ahmed wants to start an auto-repair business because he likes to work with his hands. He hopes to learn English and get a high school diploma. Then he plans to attend a trade school.

_____
_____
_____
_____

You may already be familiar with online English classes, but did you know you can earn an Associate degree, BA / BS, or even a Master's degree online? These are great, flexible options for adults balancing work, family, and long-term goals.

LESSON 3

Workplace Goals

GOAL ▶ Set work goals

A Listen to and read about Carmen's work goals.

> Carmen has many goals. She wants to have a career. She wants to be a counselor in an adult school or a college because she wants to help people. She needs to go to school for many years to study, but first she needs to learn English. She will go to Clear Mountain Adult School for two more years. She is going to learn English and get a GED. Carmen also needs to work. She needs a part-time job now, and later she plans to work at a school for more experience.

B **INTERPRET** Study the timeline and talk about Carmen's plans with a partner.

Carmen's Plan					
Year 1	Year 3	Year 4	Year 5	Year 7	Year 9
Go to Clear Mountain Adult School Get a part-time job	Get a high school diploma Start Mountain Heights Community College	Get a part-time job as a teacher's aide	Transfer to a university	Get a part-time job in the career office of the university	Graduate from the university with a BA degree Get a job as a counselor

EXAMPLE: Student A: What does Carmen plan to do in year 1?
           Student B: She plans to go to Clear Mountain Adult School and get a part-time job.

It's never too late to continue your education.

C Study the charts with your classmates and teacher.

Future: Will			
Subject	Will	Base Verb	Information
I / You / He / She / It / We / They	will	go	to school for two more years.
		study	English this year.

Future: Be Going To			
Subject	Be going to	Base Verb	Information
I	am going to	get	a GED.
You / They	are going to	study	medicine.
He / She / It	is going to	go	to college.
Use *will* for something you hope to do in the future or for a promise. Use *be going to* for definite plans for the future.			

D **COMPARE** Look at the diagram and write sentences about Carmen's and Kossi's future plans. Use either *will* or *be going to*.

Carmen
- get a GED
- become a teacher's aide
- become a counselor

Carmen and Kossi
- work part-time
- study English
- go to college
- get a college degree

Kossi
- get an Associate degree in Science
- become a pediatrician

1. Carmen is going to become a counselor.
2. _____
3. _____
4. _____
5. _____
6. _____

LESSON 3 205

E PREDICT What does Ahmed do? What do you think his plan is?

F INTERPRET Read Ahmed's timeline.

Ahmed's Plan			
Year 1	Year 2	Year 3	Year 4
Go to Clear Mountain Adult School	Get a part-time job in an automobile shop	Go to a community college and study auto mechanics and accounting	Start an auto-repair business

G PREDICT Match the statements to the reasons. Then listen and check your answers.

_____ 1. Ahmed wants to get a part-time job in an automobile shop

_____ 2. Ahmed needs to start his auto-repair business

_____ 3. Ahmed needs to go to Clear Mountain Adult School

_____ 4. Ahmed plans to go to a community college

a. because he wants to be self-employed.

b. because he wants to study auto mechanics and accounting.

c. because he wants to learn English.

d. because he wants experience in auto repair.

H PLAN Write a work goal. Use *because* and write why you want to reach this goal.

_____

_____

206 UNIT 8

LESSON 4

Lifelong Learning
GOAL ▶ Solve problems

A PREDICT Why isn't Gonzalo sitting with the other students? How does he feel?

B Read Gonzalo's story. 🎧

Gonzalo's first day at Eastwood Adult School was difficult. He didn't speak English, and many students only spoke Spanish or Portuguese. He wanted to go home, but he didn't. He went to school every day. He worked hard and listened carefully. Now he can speak and understand English.

C SOLVE Look at Gonzalo's problems and find the solutions. Match the problem to the solution. There is more than one solution for every problem.

Problems

_____ 1. didn't speak English

_____ 2. wanted a high school diploma

_____ 3. wanted to go to the library

_____ 4. didn't have a job

Solutions

a. asked a friend for help

b. looked online

c. went to school every day

d. worked hard and listened carefully

e. called for the address

f. looked on a map

g. talked to a counselor

h. took online courses

D Study the charts with your classmates and teacher.

Because		
Statement		**Reason or Problem**
Carmen plans to go to college They hope to go to an adult school She asked for help He asked a friend	because	she wants to be a nurse. they want to learn English. she didn't speak English. he didn't have a job.

So		
Reason or Problem		**Statement**
Carmen wants to be a nurse, They want to learn English, She didn't speak English, He didn't have a job,	so	she plans to go to college. they hope to go to an adult school. she asked for help. he asked a friend.

E **PREDICT** Predict what Gonzalo did to resolve his problems. Then listen and check your answers.

Problem	Ask a friend / neighbor	Talk to the police	Go to school	Look online	Go to the library	Talk to a counselor	Ask the teacher
1. He didn't speak English.	X		X		X		
2. He didn't have a job.							
3. He didn't know where to find information about citizenship.							
4. He needed to find a home for his family.							
5. He needed to find a school for his children.							
6. He didn't know what to do in an emergency.							

F On a separate piece of paper, write sentences about Gonzalo. Use *so*.

EXAMPLE: *Gonzalo didn't speak English, so he went to school.*

G Match the resource with the way it can help. There can be more than one answer.

_____ 1. the public library   a. give advice on health and legal problems

_____ 2. the internet   b. lend books or videos

_____ 3. help line   c. offer classes in English, computer programming, or art

_____ 4. an adult education center   d. give information about the latest news and job posts

H **INTERPRET** Read the flyer.

Mountain View Public Library

Monday-Thursday: 9:00 a.m.–9 p.m.
Friday-Saturday: 9 a.m.–5 p.m.
Sunday: 1 p.m.–5:00 p.m.

The Mountain View Public Library has books for adults and children of every age. Our collection includes books in more than 40 languages, available online or in print.

Kids are always welcome to come for story hour and our clay time fun group. Adults can take one of our ESL or citizenship classes, or join us for our monthly Adult Book Club discussions.

For more information, check our website or come to the information desk at the main entrance. Our services are free to all state residents.

I List the things you can do at the Mountain View Public Library.

1. *You can borrow books.*
2. _____
3. _____
4. _____

J **APPLY** Tell a group where you go for help when you have a problem. Look at E for examples of problems.

LESSON 4

LESSON 5

My Goals

GOAL ▸ Write down goals

A INFER Look at the pictures. What are Marie's plans in each picture?

1. _____

2. _____

3. _____

4. _____

B Listen and write the sentences in order. 🎧

First, _Marie plans to study nursing and work part-time as a home health aide_____.

Second, _____.

Third, _____.

Fourth, _____.

C Read the goals below. Check (✓) any goals you have.

- ☐ buy a house
- ☐ keep a job
- ☐ participate in child's school
- ☐ get married
- ☐ learn new skills at work
- ☐ get a high school diploma
- ☐ have children
- ☐ get a promotion
- ☐ go to college
- ☐ become a citizen
- ☐ get a better job
- ☐ graduate from college
- ☐ get a job
- ☐ study English

D **COMPARE** Work with a partner. Complete the diagram.

My goals | **Our goals** | **My partner's goals**

Some people plan to become citizens of the United States.

LESSON 5 211

E Study the paragraph and the correct formatting with your classmates and teacher.

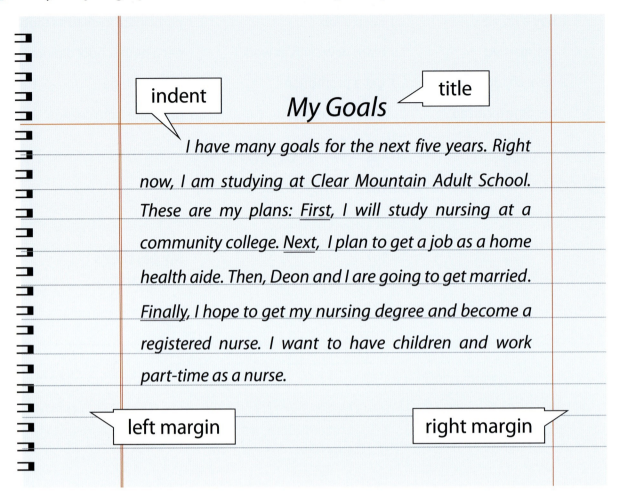

F Read the paragraph again. Look at the underlined words. What do they show?

G PLAN Write your plans for the next five years.

First, I _____.

Next, _____.

Then, _____.

Finally, _____.

H CREATE Write a paragraph about your goals. Use the example paragraph in E as a model. When you are finished, share it with the class.

LESSON 6 — Explore the Workforce

GOAL ▸ Explore employment opportunities in education

A Read about the cost of living and study the map. 🎧

In the United States, the cost of living is different from state to state. Cost of living is a calculation of the cost of things like housing, food, utilities, and other items people need to live every day. Most of the time, salaries are higher when the cost of living is higher. Within a state, the cost of living is often higher in big cities than outside mostly because of housing costs. Many colleges and universities are in big cities.

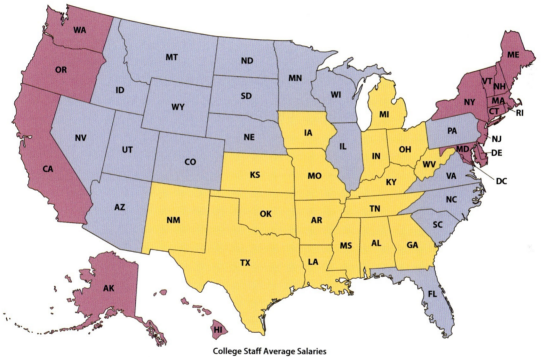

College Staff Average Salaries

	Teacher's Aide	Counselor	English Professor	Dean
Low Cost of Living	$52,012	$64,916	$90,707	$101,166
Average Cost of Living	$52,577	$67,942	$91,682	$106,890
High Cost of Living	$55,056	$75,486	$99,291	$116,681

B In your notebook, answer the questions about the map.

1. How much does an English teacher earn in states with high cost of living?

2. Compared to a high cost of living state, how much less does a counselor make in a low cost of living state?

3. Name three states with: a) a low cost of living, b) an average cost of living, and c) a high cost of living.

LESSON 6 213

C Work in a group. Discuss which states you think have the best financial benefits for educators. Share your ideas with the class.

D Listen and choose all the statements that are true about counselors.

☐ Counselors do students' homework for them.
☐ Counselors answer questions about classes at the school.
☐ Counselors help students' social skills.
☐ Counselors on average make over $60,000 a year.
☐ Counselors need only an Associate degree.
☐ Counselors need only a Bachelor's degree.
☐ Counselors usually need a Master's degree.
☐ Most states require counselors to get a credential or certificate.
☐ Most of the time, counselors work alone to get experience.
☐ Counselors often work with other counselors in internships to get experience.
☐ Counselors need analytical skills and compassion.
☐ Counselors need skills in sports to be successful.
☐ Counselors need good communication skills.

E Complete the outline of the listening using the statements from **D**.

I. Introduction

a. Counselors help students answer questions about school.

b. _____

c. _____

II. Education & Requirements

a. _____

b. _____

c. _____

III. Skills

a. _____

b. _____

F Describe to a partner what a counselor is and what a counselor can do. Use **E** to help you.

G This counselor from a Community College is talking to a prospective student and a parent. Work with a partner. Discuss with a partner what you learned about a counselor position. Do you think you could do the work of this counselor with the right education?

H **REFLECT** Check what is true about you.

☐ I am friendly.　　　　　　　　☐ I am persuasive.

☐ I am a people person.　　　　　☐ I like speaking in front of people.

☐ I like spending time with others.　☐ I am compassionate.

☐ I am organized.　　　　　　　☐ I like to help others.

I **INVESTIGATE** In a group, follow the steps, and research educational careers.

1. Go to your favorite search engine.

2. Type "educational careers."

3. Open at least three websites.

4. Write five new things you learn.

1. _____
2. _____
3. _____
4. _____
5. _____

J Choose a job title related to education. Go to a job search site online and see if there are any openings within 50 miles of your school or home. What is the job with the most posts?

LESSON 6　215

Review

A Use the words to complete the paragraph.

| Associate | Bachelor's | community | diploma | elementary |

Children in the United States start _____ school at five or six years old. Next, they usually go to a junior high school or middle school, and then to high school. When they finish high school, they receive a (n) _____. After that, they can get a job, or go to a junior college or a (n) _____ college for two years, where they get a(n) _____ degree. They can also go to a university for four years and get a(n) _____ degree.

B Match the words with the definitions.

_____ 1. resident   a. finish high school or college

_____ 2. vocational   b. person who advises other people

_____ 3. counselor   c. related to studying

_____ 4. academic   d. person who lives in a country or state

_____ 5. graduate   e. related to your job

C Ask three classmates about their goals. Write sentences about them.

1. _____
   _____
   _____

2. _____
   _____
   _____

3. _____
   _____
   _____

Learner Log   I can set academic goals.
☐ Yes   ☐ No   ☐ Maybe

D Read about Teresa. Use the words from the box to label the parts of the paragraph.

| indent | left margin | right margin | title |

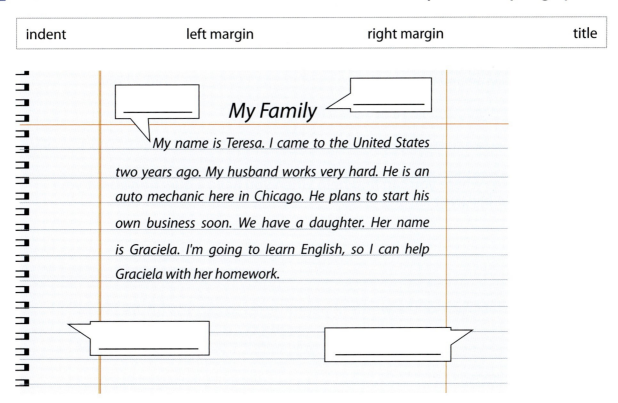

E Write a paragraph about yourself. Use *plan to, hope to, want to, going to,* and *will* to talk about your future plans. Choose one of the titles below.

1. My Family   2. My Job   3. My Goals

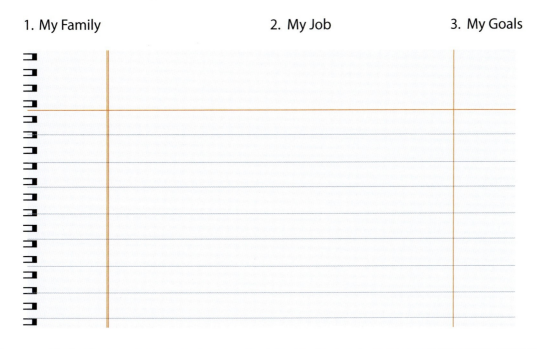

Learner Log I can write down goals.
　　Yes　　No　　Maybe

Review

F Read the goals and write *P / F* for personal or family goals, *V* for vocational goals, or *A* for academic goals.

1. __A__ get a high school diploma
2. _____ travel around the world
3. _____ learn programming at a trade school
4. _____ have two children
5. _____ get a part-time job
6. _____ buy a house
7. _____ read a novel
8. _____ work in a doctor's office

G List resources where you can find help when you have a question about your education and career.

_____   _____

_____   _____

H Use the correct form of the words in parentheses to express future plans.

1. Kimberly _____ (will) work in a doctor's office someday.
2. Paul and Kimberly _____ (be going to) have a baby.
3. She _____ (hope to) finish school before the baby comes.
4. He _____ (want to) get a better job before the baby comes.
5. They _____ (plan to) build a new baby's room in their home.

I Complete the sentences about yourself.

1. I want to _____.
2. I hope to _____.
3. I plan to _____.
4. I am going to _____.
5. I will _____.

Learner Log	I can identify goals. ☐ Yes ☐ No ☐ Maybe	I can set work goals. ☐ Yes ☐ No ☐ Maybe	I can solve problems. ☐ Yes ☐ No ☐ Maybe

Team Project

Make a Timeline
SOFT SKILL ▶ Presentation Skills

In a group, you are going to make a timeline of your goals.

1. Form a team of three or four students.
2. Draw a timeline for your group for the next five years.
3. Each team member writes three goals on pieces of paper and puts them on the timeline.
4. Show your timeline to the other groups.

Portfolio

You are going to write a paragraph and make a timeline of your goals to include in your personal portfolio.

1. Make a timeline on a large piece of paper. On your timeline, write what you want to do for the next five years.
2. Write a paragraph about your family.
3. Write a paragraph about what you are doing now in your life.
4. Write a paragraph about your plans for the next five years.
5. Show your paragraphs to a partner and ask for comments. Use the comments to improve your writing.
6. Make a cover sheet for your timeline and your paragraphs.
7. Present your portfolio to the class and read your paragraphs.

PRESENTATION SKILLS
Use Technology for Presentations
Using a computer presentation program can help improve your presentation. It will also help you organize your ideas. For example, here is one way you can organize a presentation for this project.

Slide 1: Title and name of team members.
Slide 2: Team member 1 timeline and paragraph.
Slide 3–5: Other team members' timelines and paragraphs.
Slide 6: Summary of your team's work.

Tips for Preparing the Slides
1. Make sure the font size is big enough.
2. Keep the pages simple.
3. Use transitions between slides.

Tips for Presenting with Technology
1. Practice first.
2. Don't read slides. Keep eye contact with the audience as much as possible.
3. Don't block the screen.
4. Speak slowly and clearly.

Reading Challenge

A In the article, you will read about Kakenya, who needed help to reach her goal. Look up these verbs in the dictionary. How are they different?

influence, persuade, encourage, convince = to change someone's opinion

B **RANK** In a group, rank the best ways to persuade people to do something. Rank from 1–8; 1 is the best way.

_____ give examples

_____ give facts

_____ make a promise

_____ talk about benefits

_____ share your idea in writing

_____ make sure you talk to them at the right time

_____ be enthusiastic

_____ show the history

C Read Kakenya's story.

D **INFER** Answer the questions about Kakenya's story.

1. What diplomas and / or degrees did Kakenya earn?

   a. no degree or diploma   b. only a high school diploma   c. a high school diploma and college degrees

2. How old do you think Kakenya was when she convinced her father to let her go to school?

   a. 11–13   b. 14–17   c. 17–21

3. Why do you think Kakenya was confident when she returned from the United States?

   a. She liked the United States.   b. She was older.   c. She had more education.

4. How did Kakenya help her village?

   a. She started a school.   b. She learned English.   c. She didn't get married young.

E Work with a partner. Discuss your answers in **D**. Find evidence in the story for your answers. Underline it.

F In a group, talk about when you persuaded someone in your family or at work to change their opinion. How did you do it?

The Right to an Education

Kakenya Ntaiya is an educator who grew up in a village in Kenya. Many girls in her village and other villages in Kenya marry when they are 12 or 13 years old. They also don't go to high school, but Kakenya wanted an education.
5 She had to convince her father to let her go to high school because he wanted her to get married young and start a family. He gave permission and she studied in school. Then, after high school, she wanted to go to college in the United States but had to persuade everyone in the village.
10 Kakenya wanted to help the girls in her village, and she promised them that she would come back and teach them what she learned. The people in the village collected money for her to study in the US.

After she completed college, Kakenya came home confident that she could help the village. She had to encourage the people again because she wanted to build a school for girls. Kakenya
15 understands that education is important and can help everyone, and now in Kakenya's small village an elementary school and a high school that she started are making a difference in the lives of many young girls, like the students in the photo. She says, "I want this school not only to *empower** Kenya's girls, but also their mothers, fathers, and entire villages." Kakenya is an example for others to follow, and now she's teaching people who want to make a difference like her.

*****empower** make stronger or more confident

Kakenya Ntaiya

These are some of Kakenya' students.

Advice to My Younger Self

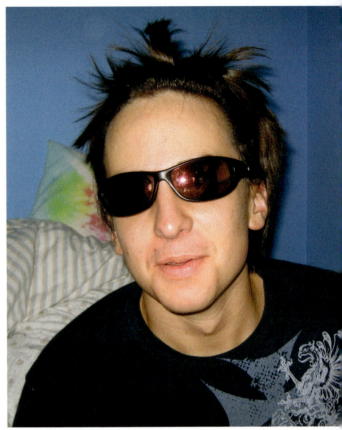

Which of these photos do you think Alex would use for his professional social media account? Why?

Before You Watch

A Work in a group. Ask and answer the questions.

1. Which social media sites or messaging apps do you use? Why do you use them?

2. Do you use social media or messaging apps differently now than you did in the past? How?

B Match each word with the correct definition.

_____ 1. crush   a. a group of people born and living during the same time

_____ 2. embarrassing   b. a feeling of sadness or disappointment about a past action

_____ 3. generation   c. hidden from others; something that only a few people know

_____ 4. post   d. a person you have strong romantic feelings for

_____ 5. regret   e. put something online so many people can see it

_____ 6. secret   f. making you feel foolish or stupid

C This video is called *Advice to My Younger Self*. Discuss with a partner what advice you think the video will give.

While You Watch

D Watch the video. Choose the correct word or phrase to complete each sentence.

1. Alex says that his generation **grew up / got hurt** with social media.

2. Alex used his away message to send secret messages to his **mom / crush**.

3. Alex learned that posting something online means **everyone / only your friends** can see it.

4. Alex thinks the photos of him at parties in college are **embarrassing / fun**.

5. Alex wishes he had **fewer / more** photos and videos of traveling in South Korea.

6. Alex says he **wants / doesn't want** to change his past.

E Watch the video again. What is NOT a piece of advice Alex gives?

1. Don't post private messages for everyone to see.
2. Don't talk to multiple friends at the same time.
3. Don't post embarrassing photos.
4. Take lots of photos, but only post a few.

After You Watch

F Work in a group. Discuss what Alex means when he says:

1. "My generation grew up with social media. I mean really *grew up*."

2. "As embarrassing as these internet life lessons were, I don't want to change the past."

G Work with a partner. Write three pieces of advice you can remember from the video. Do you follow this advice in your own life? Are there any internet life lessons you have learned?

_____

_____

_____

Life Skills Video Practice

UNIT 1 What Does He Look Like?

A BEFORE Discuss the questions with a partner.

1. You find someone's wallet on the floor. What do you do?
2. Have you ever lost an important item? If so, what did you lose?

B WHILE Write *Mr. Patel, Mateo,* or *Timothy Roberts* to show who completed the action.

1. He leaves the store. _____
2. He returns the wallet. _____
3. He directs a customer to the boy's section. _____
4. He finds a wallet. _____
5. He shakes Mr. Patel's hand. _____

C AFTER Write *1st* for the *first customer* and *2nd* for the *second customer*.

1. Which customer is in their 30s? __1st__
2. Which customer has brown pants? _____
3. Which customer has curly hair? _____
4. Which customer has a red shirt? _____

UNIT 2 Do You Have the Receipt?

A BEFORE Discuss the questions with a partner.

1. Have you ever returned an item? If you have, what was it?
2. Why did you return the item?

B WHILE Watch the video and complete the parts of the conversation.

Mrs. Smith: Well, I want to (1) _____ this sweater, but I don't have the receipt.

Mateo: Well, you can (2) _____ it for something else in the store.

Mrs. Smith: Actually … I really like that (3) _____ over there.

Mateo: Well, maybe you can exchange this (4) _____ for that blouse over there.

C AFTER Read the statements. Write *T* for true and *F* for false.

1. Hector doesn't know how to use the cash register. __T__
2. Mateo takes a break. _____
3. Mrs. Smith wants to return a green sweater. _____
4. Hector tells Mrs. Smith she is his first customer. _____
5. Mrs. Smith tells Mr. Patel she is not happy with the service at the shop. _____

UNIT 3 Let's Make a Shopping List

A BEFORE Discuss the questions with a partner.

1. When you go to the supermarket, do you make a shopping list?
2. What items do you always buy when you go to the supermarket?

B WHILE Watch the video. Choose what Mrs. Sanchez needs to buy.

- ☐ two pounds of ground beef
- ☐ a dozen eggs
- ☐ an onion
- ☐ garlic
- ☐ a green bell pepper
- ☐ ketchup
- ☐ breadcrumbs
- ☐ milk
- ☐ salt and pepper
- ☐ oregano
- ☐ basil
- ☐ ice cream

C AFTER Number the events in the correct order.

_____ Hector reminds his mother to buy ice cream.

_____ Mrs. Sanchez reads her list.

_____ Mrs. Sanchez thanks Hector.

_____ Hector agrees to help his mother with the shopping list.

_____ Hector enters the kitchen where his mother is writing a list.

UNIT 4 Every Penny Counts

A BEFORE Discuss the questions with a partner.

1. What do you spend too much money on?
2. What can you do to save money?

B WHILE Watch the video. Read the statements and write *T* for true and *F* for false.

1. Hector wants something to eat. _____
2. Mr. and Mrs. Sanchez are making a family budget. _____
3. The coffee maker breaks when Hector tries to use it. _____
4. Mr. Sanchez hopes to save money on another item so he can buy a new microwave. _____
5. Hector and his parents go shopping for a coffee maker. _____

C AFTER In your notebook write one sentence with each of the words in the box.

| budgets | earn | expenses | plan | save | spend |

UNIT 5 Where Is the Post Office?

A BEFORE Discuss the questions with a partner.

1. What can you do at the post office?
2. How do you get to the nearest post office from your home?

B WHILE Watch the video. Choose the correct words to complete directions to the post office.

1. Get (off / down) at the mall.
2. Walk (towards / away from) the library.
3. Turn (left / right) on Nutwood.
4. The post office is (on / at) the left.

C AFTER Number the events in the correct order.

_____ The man gives Naomi directions to the post office.

_____ A man sits on the bench.

__1__ Naomi is sitting by herself on the bench writing to Tara.

_____ Naomi writes that the people are very friendly.

_____ Naomi's bus arrives.

_____ The man gets on his bus.

UNIT 6 I've Got a Splitting Headache

A BEFORE Read the problems and give advice. Write your answers in your notebook.

1. I have a headache.
2. I cut my finger.
3. My stomach hurts.

B WHILE Watch the video and complete the parts of the conversation.

Hector: Mr. Patel, do we have any (1) _____?

Mr. Patel: Let me guess. Mateo has a (2) _____?

Mr. Patel: (3) _____ is a little stronger than the others.

Mateo: How much (4) _____ I take?

Mr. Patel: You (5) _____ more than six per day.

C AFTER Match each sentence with the appropriate response.

_____ 1. I have a cut.

_____ 2. I have a headache.

_____ 3. My stomach hurts.

_____ 4. I'm very tired.

a. Would you like some aspirin?

b. Take some antacid.

c. You'd better clean it with alcohol.

d. You should get some rest.

UNIT 7 Being on Time Is Very Important

A BEFORE Discuss the questions with a partner.

1. Do you like to receive constructive feedback?

2. Why do you think giving and receiving feedback is important at work?

B WHILE Watch the video and complete the parts of the conversation.

Mr. Patel: Being on (1) _____ for work is very important.

Hector: I'll work (2) _____ to get here early from now on.

Mr. Patel: That's good Hector. That's a very good (3) _____ to have.

Hector: I really am (4) _____ my best to learn all about the job.

C AFTER Match each sentence with the appropriate response.

_____ 1. I'm very pleased with your work.

_____ 2. You're late again.

_____ 3. What kinds of skills do you have?

_____ 4. We are behind schedule.

a. I'll stay late tonight and catch up.

b. I can type and enter data very fast.

c. Thank you. I try my best.

d. I'll be on time tomorrow.

UNIT 8 Sounds Like a Good Plan

A BEFORE Discuss the questions with a partner.

1. Do you set goals for yourself?

2. Describe a goal that you achieved. What did you do to achieve it?

B WHILE Watch the video and complete the parts of the conversation.

Naomi: It teaches you how to (1) _____ goals and achieve them.

Naomi: "To be (2) _____ in life, you need to set goals."

Mateo: (3) _____ give your life a sense of (4) _____.

Naomi: "First, you need to (5) _____ your goal. Then, you need to make a (6) _____ for achieving your goal."

Naomi: You have to make a plan that goes (7) _____-by-step.

C AFTER In your notebook, write the steps Naomi, Mateo, and Hector plan to take to achieve their goals.

LIFE SKILLS VIDEO PRACTICE 227

Stand Out Vocabulary List

PRE-UNIT pp. 2–11

angry
frustrated
happy
nervous
number
sad
tired

UNIT 1 pp. 12–37

actor
aunt
blizzard
brother
career
cloudy
construction engineer
daughter
dust storm
eyes
father
firestorm
flood
foggy
food scientist
granddaughter
grandfather
grandmother
grandson
hair
heavy
height
hurricane
husband
mother
nephew
niece
nurse
old
parents
rainy
salesperson
short
sister
snowy
social worker
son
sunny
tall
thin
tornado
uncle
weight
wife
windy
young

UNIT 2 pp. 38–63

baseball cap
blouse
boots
coat
commute
dress
gig worker
gloves
hustling
income
isolation
jeans
juggling
pants
parental leave
sandals
scarf
shirt
shoes
shorts
skirt
sneakers
socks
suit
sunglasses
sweater
t-shirt
tie

UNIT 3 pp. 64–89

add
baker
baking needs
beverage
boil
bottle
box
breakfast
can
canned goods
carton
chef
chop
cook
dairy
dessert
dinner
drain
earnings
frozen foods
fruit
gallon
grains
hospitality
jar
loaf
lunch
main course
meats
mix
opening
peel
pound
produce
protein
restaurant manager
salad
sandwich
side order
soup
supermarket
training
vegetables
whip

UNIT 4 pp. 90–115

apartment
architect
armchair
ATM
balcony
bathroom
bedroom
bookcase
budget
cash
coffee table
condominium
couch
deposit
dining room
dining room table
drafter
dresser
electrician
end table
expense
for sale
house
inspector
kitchen
lamp
living room
mobile home
paycheck
plumber
pool
rent
withdraw
yard

UNIT 5 pp. 118–143

arcade
bank
bowling alley
city hall
clothes store
courthouse
department store
EMT
entertainment center
fast-food restaurant
fire station
firefighter
gas station
hardware store
hospital
library
movie theater
paramedic
pharmacy
police station
post office
safety
security guard
shoe store
shopping mall
911 operator

UNIT 6 pp. 144–169

aches and pains
antacid
arm
backache
chest
cold
cough
cough syrup
dental assistant
dental hygienist
directions
ear
emergency
exceed
eye
fever
foot
hand

head
headache
health care
heart problem
high blood pressure
leg
mouth
muscle aches
neck
nose
nursing aide
orderlies
pain reliever
persist
pharmacist
physical therapist
radiologic tech
reduce
registered nurse
runny nose
shoulder
sore throat
stomach
stomachache
stress
symptoms
tablets
teenagers
the flu
tooth (teeth)
toothache
uses
warning

UNIT 7 pp. 170–195

administrative assistant
apartment manager
badge
badge reader
blood pressure monitor
cashier
commitment
computer
computer programmer
construction worker
copier
delivery person
driver
home health aide
homemaker
hotel clerk
human resources specialist
landscaper
laptop
manager
musician
payroll clerk
plug
positive attitude
printer
punctuality
purchasing manager
retail salesperson
wheelbarrow
work habits
wrench

UNIT 8 pp. 196–221

adult school
Associate Degree
Bachelor's Degree
certificate
college
community college
cost of living
counselor
dean
diploma
GED (General Equivalency Diploma)
goals
graduate
Master's Degree
professor
trade school
university

Irregular Verb List

Base Verb	Simple Past	Base Verb	Simple Past
be	was, were	give	gave
bring	brought	go	went
build	built	have	had
buy	bought	make	made
choose	chose	meet	met
come	came	put	put
do	did	read	read
drink	drank	see	saw
drive	drove	send	sent
draw	drew	sleep	slept
eat	ate	speak	spoke
feel	felt	teach	taught
find	found	write	wrote

Stand Out Grammar Reference

PRE-UNIT

The Verb Be			
Subject	Be	Feelings	Example Sentence
I	am	fine	I **am** fine. (I**'m** fine.)
You / We / They	are	nervous sad tired	You **are** nervous. (You**'re** nervous.) We **are** sad. (We**'re** sad.) They **are** tired. (They**'re** tired.)
He / She / It	is	happy angry frustrated	He **is** angry. (He**'s** angry.) She **is** frustrated. (She**'s** frustrated.)

Possessive Adjectives		
Pronoun	Possessive Adjective	Example Sentence
I	My	**My** address is 3356 Archer Blvd.
You	Your	**Your** phone number is (123) 555-5678.
He	His	**His** last name is Yang.
She	Her	**Her** first name is Lien.
It	Its	**Its** number is 10.
We	Our	**Our** teacher is Mr. Kelley.
They	Their	**Their** home is in Minneapolis.

Questions with Can			
Can	Pronoun	Verb	Example Sentence
Can	you	help speak answer repeat say spell	Can you help me? Can you speak slower? Can you answer the question? Can you repeat that, please? Can you say it again, please? Can you spell it, please?

UNIT 1

Simple Present: Be			
Subject	Verb	Information	Example Sentence
I	am	from Vietnam	I **am** from Vietnam.
We / You / They	are	single divorced	We **are** single. You **are** divorced.
He / She / It	is	23 years old	He **is** 23 years old. She **is** 23 years old.

Simple Present: Have		
Subject	Verb	Information
I / You / We / They	have	three brothers. two sisters.
He / She	has	no cousins. three sons.

Comparative and Superlative Adjectives		
Adjective	Comparative Adjective	Superlative Adjective
tall	taller	the tallest
short	shorter	the shortest
old	older	the oldest
young	younger	the youngest

Simple Present			
Subject	Verb	Information	Example Sentence
I / You / We / They	live eat go make play	in California lunch to school dinner soccer	I **live** in California. I **eat** lunch at 4:00 p.m. You **go** to school at 8:00 a.m. We sometimes **make** dinner. They **play** soccer on Saturday.
He / She / It	live**s**** eat**s*** goe**s**** make**s*** play**s****	in California lunch to school dinner soccer	She **lives** in California. He **eats** lunch at 12:00 p.m. Nadia **goes** to school at 10:00 a.m. Gilberto **makes** dinner. She **plays** soccer on Friday.

Pronunciation: */s/   **/z/

UNIT 2

Negative Simple Present			
Subject	Negative	Base Verb	
I / You / We / They	don't	wear	sandals.
He / She	doesn't		

Comparative and Superlative Adjectives		
Adjective	Comparative Adjective	Superlative Adjective
cheap	cheaper	the cheapest
expensive	more expensive	the most expensive

Present Continuous			
Subject	Be	Verb + -ing	Example Sentence
I	am	wearing	I **am wearing** a sweater right now.
You / We / They	are		We **are wearing** shoes.
He / She / It	is		She **is wearing** sunglasses today.

	Near	Not Near
Singular	this	that
Plural	these	those

UNIT 3

Questions with Can

Can	Pronoun	Base Verb	Example Question
Can	I	take help	Can I take your order? Can I help you?
Can	you		Can you take my order? Can you take our order, please? Can you help me? Can you help us?

Some / Any

Question	Do we need **any** milk?
Statement	We need **some** milk.

Count and Noncount Nouns

Count Nouns	Use *many* with nouns you can count.	How *many* tomatoes do we need? How *many* pounds of tomatoes do we need?
Noncount Nouns	Use *much* with nouns you cannot count.	How *much* flour do we need? How *much* rice do we need?

Imperatives

	Base Verb	Example Sentence
~~you~~	drain	**Drain** the water.
	chop	**Chop** the potatoes.
	peel	**Peel** the potatoes.

Negative Imperatives

	Negative	Base Verb	Example Sentence
~~you~~	do not don't	boil	**Do not boil** the water. (**Don't boil** the water.)
		use	**Do not use** salt. (**Don't use** salt.)
		cook	**Do not cook** in the microwave. (**Don't cook** in the microwave.)

UNIT 4

Information Question	Answer
How much is the house?	It's $2,500 a month.
What kind of housing is Number 2?	It's a mobile home.
Where is the condominium?	It's on Shady Glen.
How many bedrooms does the apartment have?	It has three bedrooms.

Information Questions

What is your name?	**How** long did you live there?
Where do you live now?	**Who** is your employer?
Where did you live before?	**What** is your position?

Modal: Might

Subject	Modal	Base Verb	Example Sentence
I / You / He / She / It / We / They	might	spend	We **might** spend $300 a month on food.

UNIT 5

Imperatives			
	Base Verb		Example Sentence
~~you~~	go	straight straight ahead	**Go** straight three blocks. **Go** straight ahead.
	turn	left right around	**Turn** left on Nutwood. **Turn** right on Nutwood. **Turn** around.
	stop	on the left on the right	**Stop** on the left. **Stop** on the right.

Present Continuous			
Subject	*Be*	Base Verb + *ing*	Example Sentence
I	am	writing	I **am** / I**'m writing** this letter in English.
You / We / They	are	going	We **are** / We**'re going** to the mall.
He / She / It	is	eating	He **is** / He**'s eating** at the coffee shop.

Simple Past (Regular)		
Subject	Verb (Base + *ed*)	Example Sentence
I / You / He / She / It / We / They	talked	I **talked** with Marie.
	wanted	She **wanted** a sandwich.
	walked	We **walked** in the park.

Simple Past (Irregular)		
Subject	Irregular Verb	Example Sentence
I / You / He / She / It / We / They	went (go)	I **went** to the park.
	ate (eat)	She **ate** at the coffee shop.
	bought (buy)	We **bought** new dresses.
	send (sent)	They **sent** a letter.

GRAMMAR REFERENCE

UNIT 6

Adjective	Comparative Adjective	Superlative Adjective
serious	more serious less serious	the most serious the least serious
common	more common less common	the most common the least common

Simple Past (Regular)	
Subject	Verb (Base + *ed*)
I / You	walked.* (walk)
He / She / It	talked.* (talk)
We / They	smoked.* (smoke) played.* (play) waited.* (wait)

Simple Past (Irregular)	
Subject	Verb
I / You,	had (have)
He / She / It	went (go)
We / They	said (say)

Simple Past: *Be*		
Subject	Be	Example Sentence
I / He / She / It	was	I **was** sick.
You / We / They	were	You **were** at the hospital.

Infinitives		
Subject	Verb	*to* + Base Verb
I	need	to exercise.

Modal: *Should*			
Subject	*Should*	Base Verb	Example Sentence
I	should shouldn't	take	I **should** take two tablets.
You			chew	You **shouldn't** chew this tablet.
He / She / It			drink	He **shouldn't** drink alcohol with this medicine. She **should** take this medicine for a headache.
It			hurt	It **shouldn't** hurt.
We / They			swallow	They **should** swallow this tablet with water.

Ask and Answer with *Be* (Past)			
	Subject	*Be* Verb	
Question	What	was	the most common profession in 2008?
Answer	Registered nurse	was	the most common profession.
Question	What	were	the professions with pay between 60k and 80k?

234 GRAMMAR REFERENCE

UNIT 7

Future: Will (Affirmative)			
Subject	Will	Base Verb	Example Sentence
I	will	come	I **will come** to class on time.
You		listen	You **will listen** carefully and follow directions.
He		work	He **will work** hard.
She		understand	She **will understand** the job.
It		help	It **will help**.
We		have	We **will have** a positive attitude.
They		do	They **will do** their homework.

Future: Will (Negative)			
Subject	Will	Base Verb	Example Sentence
I / You	will not (won't)	come	I **won't come** to class late.
He / She		leave	He **won't leave** class early.
It		help	It **won't help**.
We / They		forget	We **will not forget** our homework.

Can	Can't
I **can** type.	I **can't** type.
He **can** type.	He **can't** type.

Simple Past (Regular)	
Subject	Past Verb (Base + -ed)
I / You / He / She / It / We / They	checked. worked. cooked.

Simple Past: Be	
Subject	Be
I / He / She / It	was.
We / You / They	were.

Negative Simple Past (Regular)		
Subject	Did + not	Base verb
I / You / He / She / It / We / They	did not (didn't)	check. work. cook.

Negative Simple Past: Be	
Subject	Be + not
I / He / She / It	was not (wasn't).
We / You / They	were not (weren't).

Imperatives		
~~you~~	Base Verb	Example Sentence
	open follow print	Open the document. Follow the instructions on your computer screen. Print your document.

UNIT 8

Future Plans: *Want to, Hope to, Plan to*		
Subject	Verb	Infinitive (*to* + Base)
I / You / We / They	hope, want, plan	to study in school for three years.
He / She / It	hopes, wants, plans	to graduate from college. to get married.

Future Plans: *Be Going to*		
Subject	*Be Going to*	Base Verb
I	am going to	get a high school diploma.
You / We / They	are going to	participate in class.
He / She / It	is going to	buy a house.

Because			
Statement	Reason		
	Because	Subject + Verb	Information
Marie plans to go to college	because	she wants	to be a nurse.
Lien hopes to learn English		she plans	to go to college.
They hope to go to an adult school		they want	to learn English.
I want to go to a trade school		I want	to be a mechanic.

Future: Will

Subject	Will	Base Verb	Information
I / You / He / She / It / We / They	will	go	to school for two more years.
		study	English this year.

Future: Be Going to

Subject	Be going to	Base Verb	Information
I	am going to	take	the GED.
You / They	are going to	study	medicine.
He / She / It	is going to	go	to college.

Use *will* for something you hope to do in the future or for a promise.
Use *be going to* for definite plans for the future.

Because

Statement		Reason or Problem
Carmen plans to go to college They hope to go to an adult school She asked for help He asked a friend	because	she wants to be a nurse. they want to learn English. she didn't speak English. he didn't have a job.

So

Reason or Problem		Statement
Carmen wants to be a nurse, They want to learn English, She didn't speak English, He didn't have a job,	so	she plans to go to college. they hope to go to an adult school. she asked for help. he asked a friend.

Credits

ILLUSTRATIONS: Illustrations created by Oscar Hernandez. All illustrations and graphics are owned by © Cengage Learning, Inc.

PHOTOS: v (tl) © Charlie Zevon, (tr) © Priscilla Caraveo; **2** (tr) © Chris Crisman Photography, (cl) © shapecharge/Getty Images, (cc) © Brian Doben Photography, (cr) © Christopher Payne / Esto, (bl) © Brian Doben Photography, (bc) © Christopher Payne / Esto, (br) © Chris Crisman Photography; **3** SDI Productions/iStock/Getty Images; **4** (tl) AaronAmat/iStock/Getty Images, (tc) Fizkes/Shutterstock.com, (tr) Wayhome Studio/Shutterstock.com, (cl) Eyecrave/E+/Getty Images, (c) Antonio Guillem Fernández/Alamy Stock Photo, (cr) The Good Brigade/DigitalVision/Getty Images; **7** Agefotostock/Alamy Stock Photo; **9** (tr) Pol Solé/Alamy Stock Photo; **10** Rido/Shutterstock.com; **12–13** Frieder Blickle/laif/Redux; **14** (t) The_Pixel/Shutterstock.com, (tl) AJR_photo/Shutterstock.com; (tc) Daniel M Ernst/Shutterstock.com, (tr) Monkey Business Images/Shutterstock.com; **15** (cl1) Daniel M Ernst/Shutterstock.com, (cl2) Monkey Business Images/Shutterstock.com, (cr1) AJR_photo/Shutterstock.com, (cr2) Nadofotos/iStock/Getty Images; **17** (cl) Elizabeth Fernandez/Moment/Getty Images, (cr) FG Trade/E+/Getty Images, (bl1) Krakenimages.com/Shutterstock.com, (bl2) AJR_photo/Shutterstock.com, (bl3) El Nariz/Shutterstock.com, (bl4) Monkey Business Images/Shutterstock.com, (br1) Ranta Images/Shutterstock.com, (br2) Andy Dean Photography/Shutterstock.com, (br3) Morsa Images/DigitalVision/Getty Images, (br4) Littlekidmoment/Shutterstock.com, (br5) ESB Professional/Shutterstock.com; **18** (tl1)(tr) FG Trade/E+/Getty Images, (tl2)(cl)(bl) Monkey Business Images/Shutterstock.com, (tr)(cr) Elizabeth Fernandez/Moment/Getty Images, (br) Krakenimages.com/Shutterstock.com, (cl) AJR_photo/Shutterstock.com, (cr) Littlekidmoment/Shutterstock.com, (bl) Morsa Images/DigitalVision/Getty Images, (br) ESB Professional/Shutterstock.com; **28** (tl) Dreef/iStock/Getty Images; (tc) Jason Persoff Stormdoctor/Image Source/Getty Images, (tr) Warren Faidley/Corbis/Getty Images, (cl) MLGXYZ/Moment/Getty Images, (c) Mkfilm/Shutterstock.com, (cr) John Sirlin/EyeEm/Getty Images; **32** (tl) FatCamera/E+/Getty Images, (tr) Morsa Images/DigitalVision/Getty Images; **33** (tl1) Pekic/E+/Getty Images, (tl2) Morsa Images/DigitalVision/Getty Images, (tl3) AJR_photo/Shutterstock.com, (tr1) Blend Images - John Lund/Sam Diephuis/Getty Images, (tr2) Fizkes/Shutterstock.com, (tr3) Linda Raymond/Moment/Getty Images, (cl) Elina/Shutterstock.com, (cr1) Rouzes/E+/Getty Images, (cr2) Daniela Solomon/Moment/Getty Images; **37** Gukzilla/Shutterstock.com; **38-39** Homer Sykes/Alamy Stock Photo; **42** (cl) Morsa Images/DigitalVision/Getty Images, (cr) Oliver Rossi/Stone/Getty Images; **45** Allesalltag/Alamy Stock Photo; **49** (tc) Michaeljung/Shutterstock.com, (tc) Sean Locke Photography/Shutterstock.com, (c) Marynka Mandarinka/Shutterstock.com, (c) Optimarc/Shutterstock.com; **52** Hispanolistic/E+/Getty Images; **57** © Johanna Siegmann; **63** (t) © Bayeté Ross Smith, (c) © Bayeté Ross Smith; **64-65** © Corey Arnold/National Geographic Image Collection; **66** Minerva Studio/Shutterstock.com; **67** (tl) Dan Kosmayer/Shutterstock.com, (tr) Tadeusz Wejkszo/Shutterstock.com; **70** (tl1) Gts/Shutterstock.com, (tl2) Gts/Shutterstock.com, (tr1) Svetlana Foote/Shutterstock.com, (tr2) Africa Studio/Shutterstock.com, (cl1) Diana Taliun/Shutterstock.com, (cl2) Nexus 7/Shutterstock.com, (cr1) Vadarshop/Shutterstock.com, (cr2) Photo Melon/Shutterstock.com; **71** Elena Shashkina/Shutterstock.com; **72** (tl) 8th.creator/Shutterstock.com, (tc) The Toidi/Shutterstock.com, (tr) SOPA Images/LightRocket/Getty Images, (cl) Jeff Greenberg/Universal Images Group/Getty Images, (c) Michael Warwick/Shutterstock.com, (cr) Erik Isakson/Tetra images/Getty Images; **75** Choose myplate.gov; **76** (tl) Tetra Images, LLC/Alamy Stock Photo, (tr) Caterina Bernardi/The Image Bank/Getty Images, (cl) Bananastock/Jupiter Images, (cr) Baoba Images/Riser/Getty Images, (bl) Minerva Studio/iStock/Getty Images Plus/Getty Images; **78** Chatham172/Shutterstock.com; **79** (tr) Tatjana Baibakova/Shutterstock.com; **83** Hinterhaus Productions/DigitalVision/Getty Images; **84** (tl) Liv friis-larsen/Shutterstock.com, (tr) Photokin/Shutterstock.com, (cl) Brent Hofacker/Shutterstock.com, (cr) Vezzani Photography/Shutterstock.com; **85** (cl1) Gts/Shutterstock.com, (cl2) Svetlana Foote/Shutterstock.com, (cr1) Diana Taliun/Shutterstock.com, (cr2) Africa Studio/Shutterstock.com, (bl1) Nexus 7/Shutterstock.com, (bl2) Photo Melon/Shutterstock.com, (br1) Vadarshop/Shutterstock.com, (br2) Gts/Shutterstock.com; **86** Nelea33/Shutterstock.com; **89** Mauritius images GmbH/Alamy Stock Photo; **90-91** © Trisha Krauss; **93** (cl) Pbk-pg/Shutterstock.com, (cr) Konstantin L/Shutterstock.com, (bl) Iriana Shiyan/Shutterstock.com, (br) Atlaspix/Shutterstock.com; **94** (tl) Alihan Usullu/E+/Getty Images, (tr) Fizkes/Shutterstock.com; **95** (tl) Frank Fennema/Shutterstock.com, (tr) Tetra Images, LLC/Alamy Stock Photo, (cl) Ivan Hunter/DigitalVision/Getty Images, (cr) Kimberlymillerphoto/iStock/Getty Images; **102** (tl1) Ad Oculos/Shutterstock.com, (tl2) StudioSmart/Shutterstock.com, (tr1) Lynnette/Shutterstock.com, (tr2) Room27/Shutterstock.com, (cl1) Sandratsky Dmitriy/Shutterstock.com, (cl2) Donatas1205/Shutterstock.com, (cr1) Zhukova Valentyna/Shutterstock.com, (cr2) James Marvin Phelps/Shutterstock.com; **103** Artazum/Shutterstock.com; **109** Don Mason/Tetra images/Getty Images; **111** Paul Maguire/Shutterstock.com; **115** Dave Kaup/AFP/Getty Images; **116** KatarzynaBialasiewicz/iStock/Getty Images; **118-119** Demetrius Freeman/The New York Times/Redux; **120** Travis houston/Shutterstock.com; **122** (cl) Volodymyr Kyryliuk/Shutterstock.com, (c) Bauhaus1000/E+/Getty Images, (cr) Serhii Chrucky/Alamy Stock Photo; **136** Digital Storm/Shutterstock.com; **137** AP Images/Noah Berger; **143** (b) Jeffrey Isaac Greenberg 5+/Alamy Stock Photo; **144-145** MediaNews Group/Boulder Daily Camera via Getty Images/Getty Images; **146** (tr1) Thomas Barwick/DigitalVision/Getty Images, (tr2) Fizkes/Shutterstock.com, (cr1) NicolasMcComber/E+/Getty Images, (cr2) Vlad Teodor/Shutterstock.com; **147** Fizkes/iStock/Getty Images; **149** John Lamb/The Image Bank/Getty Images; **150** (tl1) Svetikd/E+/Getty Images, (tl2) Klebercordeiro/iStock/Getty Images, (tc) Jelena Stanojkovic/iStock/Getty Images, (tr1) Ljubaphoto/E+/Getty Images, (tr2) Thianchai sitthikongsak/Moment/Getty Images; **153** Jeffrey Isaac Greenberg 8+/Alamy Stock Photo; **156** LianeM/Alamy Stock Photo; **158** (tl) Hinterhaus Productions/DigitalVision/Getty Images, (tc) SmoothSailing/Shutterstock.com, (tr) Boonchai Wedmakawand/Moment/Getty Images; **159** (bl) Peter Dazeley/The Image Bank/Getty Images, (bc) Science Photo Library/Getty Images, (br) Moyo Studio/E+/Getty Images; **163** NurPhoto/Getty Images; **164** Photobac/Shutterstock.com; **165** (tl1) NicolasMcComber/E+/Getty Images, (tl2) Thomas Barwick/DigitalVision/Getty Images, (tr1) Fizkes/Shutterstock.com, (tr2) Vlad Teodor/Shutterstock.com; **166** (cl) Svetikd/E+/Getty Images, (cr) Ljubaphoto/E+/Getty Images, (bl) Klebercordeiro/iStock/Getty Images, (br) Moyo Studio/E+/Getty Images; **169** © Renan Ozturk; **170-171** Bill Pugliano/Getty Images News/Getty Images; **172** Michaeljung/Shutterstock.com; **175** (tl1) Susumu Yoshioka/DigitalVision/Getty Images, (tl2) Lane Oatey/Blue Jean Images/Getty Images, (tr1) Pramote Polyamate/Alamy Stock Photo, (tr2) Hero Images Inc./Alamy Stock Photo, (bl1) Krakenimages.com/Shutterstock.com, (bl2) Westend61 GmbH/Alamy Stock Photo, (br1) SolStock/E+/Getty Images, (br2) Cathy Melloan/Alamy Stock Photo; **176** (tl1) Romiri/Shutterstock.com, (tl2) Lotus studio/Shutterstock.com, (tr1) 3d_man/Shutterstock.com, (tr2) Skocko/Shutterstock.com; **185** (tl) 7th Son Studio/Shutterstock.com, (tc) Tascha Rassadornyindee/EyeEm/Getty Images, (tr) Daboost/Shutterstock.com; **191** (tl) 7th Son Studio/Shutterstock.com, (tc) Tascha Rassadornyindee/EyeEm/Getty Images, (tr) Daboost/Shutterstock.com; **192** (tl) Westend61 GmbH/Alamy Stock Photo, (tc) Pramote Polyamate/Alamy Stock Photo, (tr) Lane Oatey/Blue Jean Images/Getty Images, (cl) SolStock/E+/Getty Images, (c) Krakenimages.com/Shutterstock.com, (cr) Cathy Melloan/Alamy Stock Photo; **195** (cl) © MiraCosta College, (bc) © MiraCosta College; **196-197** Drew Angerer/Getty Images News/Getty Images; **204** Digital Vision/Getty Images; **206** South_agency/E+/Getty Images; **207** BearFotos/Shutterstock.com; **211** SDI Productions/E+/Getty Images; **215** Jeff Roberson/AP/Shutterstock.com; **221** (tr) © Kakenya Ntaiya, (b) © Kakenya Ntaiya; **222** (tl) (tr) © Alex Sigrist; **242** © NG Maps/National Geographic Image Collection.

Stand Out Skills Index

ACADEMIC SKILLS

Active Listening, 35, 61, 87, 113, 141, 167, 193, 219

Charts, graphs, and maps, 5, 8, 11, 14, 16, 19, 21, 22, 25, 26, 27, 42, 44, 47, 51, 53, 68, 70, 71, 72, 80, 81, 82, 93, 94, 99, 106, 107, 120–121, 124–127, 130, 134, 135, 138, 148, 151, 152, 157, 158, 159, 160, 161, 174, 177, 183, 186, 187, 200, 201, 203, 205, 208, 213

Collaboration, 35, 61, 87, 113, 141, 167, 193, 219

Critical thinking
    Analyze, 21, 81, 121, 161
    Apply, 8, 19, 22, 25, 45, 48, 71, 77, 97, 100, 123, 128, 131, 134, 148, 157, 180, 186, 209
    Brainstorm, 74
    Calculate, 43, 50, 67, 103, 105
    Cite, 135
    Clarify, 11
    Classify, 15, 40, 41, 72, 75, 82, 96, 98, 122, 125, 132, 147, 150, 176, 199
    Collaborate, 179
    Compare, 22, 44, 51, 62, 77, 205, 211
    Create, 19, 54, 68, 80, 94, 97, 131, 183, 212
    Define, 88, 155
    Discuss, 58
    Distinguish, 52
    Evaluate, 172
    Identify, 42, 46, 70, 147, 149, 156, 158, 159, 175, 184
    Infer, 36, 62, 130, 135, 136, 140, 210, 220
    Interpret, 6, 17, 22, 24, 29, 31, 45, 50, 55, 56, 67, 73, 75, 78, 81, 93, 96, 99, 101, 104, 107, 120, 124, 125, 126, 155, 161, 173, 177, 178, 187, 201, 204, 206, 209
    Investigate, 56, 57, 83, 109, 137, 162, 163, 189, 215
    List, 151, 172
    Organize, 44
    Plan, 71, 102, 106, 174, 200, 201, 203, 206, 212
    Predict, 3, 10, 23, 40, 49, 66, 69, 74, 92, 98, 104, 123, 131, 147, 148, 153, 157, 206, 207, 208
    Rank, 76, 151, 173, 198, 220
    Reflect, 31, 109, 137, 163, 189, 215
    Research, 27
    Self-evaluate, 57, 83
    Sequence, 79, 80, 133, 184
    Solve, 182, 207
    Survey, 5, 16, 88, 94, 95, 146, 160

Diagrams, 77, 205, 211

Grammar
    Advice, 160
    Because, 203, 208
    Comparative adjectives, 22, 44, 135, 151
    Count and noncount nouns, 71
    Future tense, 174, 200, 205
    How much and *How many*, 78
    Imperatives, 80, 127, 186
    Infinitives, 148
    Information questions, 93, 99, 107, 121
    Modals, 106, 157, 177
    Negative imperatives, 80
    Possessive adjectives, 8
    Present continuous, 47, 128
    Questions with *can*, 11, 68
    Simple past, 134, 152, 159, 183
    Simple present, 16, 25, 42, 72, 124, 130
    So, 208
    Some / any questions, 70
    Superlative adjectives, 22, 44, 81, 135, 151
    these / those, 53
    this / that, 53

Group activities, 5, 16, 35, 42, 61, 74, 97, 113, 141, 142, 146, 151, 167, 186, 193, 219

Listening
    Classified ads, 95, 101
    Conversations, 3, 6, 7, 10, 15, 23, 44, 52, 54, 67, 74, 98, 125, 127, 133, 150, 153, 154, 157, 159, 173, 177, 179, 181
    Descriptions, 95, 101
    Directions, 127, 128, 138
    Doctor's appointments, 153, 154
    Educational choices, 201, 202
    Emergencies, 159
    Food orders, 67
    Goals, 198, 199, 204, 206
    Greetings, 3–4
    Housing, 92, 98
    Instructions, 10, 11, 80, 133, 184
    Job interviews, 177, 181
    Numbers, 7
    Nutrition, 75
    Prices, 42
    Schedules, 23

Matching
    Ailments, 150
    Medical labels, 155
    Words and definitions, 104, 114, 182, 187
    Words and pictures, 102, 149, 150, 158, 175, 184, 185

Partner activities, 4, 8, 9, 15, 21, 23, 25, 44, 70, 77, 81, 106, 125, 126, 135, 154, 174, 177, 211, 214

Presentation, 35, 61, 87, 113, 141, 167, 193, 219

Pronunciation
    Clarification words, 74
    /m/ sound, 4
    Past tense, 152
    Plurals, 70
    Question intonation, 15
    Rhythm, 73
    Stress, 179
    Stress and rhythm, 93
    Yes / No questions, 11

Reading
    Advertisements, 49, 55, 56
    Ailments, 150
    Budgets, 104
    Bus schedules, 121
    Calendars, 24
    Charts, 75, 81, 158, 161, 162
    Classified ads, 93, 96–98, 101, 178
    Descriptions, 22
    Directions, 127
    Directories, 73
    Directory index, 124–125
    Emergencies, 158

Envelopes, 132
Evaluations, 173
Family relationships, 17
Flyers, 209
Goals, 198, 199, 204, 212
Health, 147
Housing, 87, 88, 95
Job applications, 177, 180
Job interviews, 181, 182
Maps, 121, 126, 127, 138
Medical labels, 155
Menus, 67, 84
Messages and letters, 129–133, 139
Receipts, 43, 48, 55
Recipes, 78–79, 86
Shopping lists, 70

Speaking
Advice, 160
Answering questions, 134, 140, 198
Asking questions, 18, 25, 27, 93, 107, 133, 162, 216
Budgets, 105
Clarification phrases, 10
Conversations, 49, 53, 68, 70, 72, 73, 78, 174, 175
Doctor's appointments, 154
Emergencies, 159
Greetings, 3–5
Interviews, 183
Personal information, 14–16

Vocabulary
Ailments, 150
because, 191
Body parts, 149
Clothing, 41, 43, 46
Community, 118, 122, 124, 125
Descriptions, 20
Education, 201–202
Emergencies, 158, 159
Family relationships, 18
Feelings, 4
Food, 66
Furniture, 102
Housing, 93, 95
Instructions, 9, 185
Jobs and careers, 29, 55, 81, 107, 135, 161, 175, 176, 178, 204
Medical labels, 155
Numbers, 7
Office equipment, 184, 185

Parts of a letter, 133
Recipes, 78
Weather, 26

Writing
Advice, 160
Answering questions, 99, 187
Budgets, 105, 106
Charts, 72, 74, 77, 81, 86
Clothing, 58
Descriptions, 20, 22, 31
Directions, 128
Family relationships, 17
Future plans, 174
Goals, 148, 200, 203, 206, 212
Imperatives, 186
Job skills, 177
Letters, 131–132
Numbers, 7
Paragraphs, 134, 203, 212
Past tense, 134
Personal information, 14
Possessive adjectives, 8
Prepositions, 126, 129
Questions, 71
Registration forms, 6, 8
Sentences, 30, 47–48, 60, 129, 130, 131, 148, 157, 161, 177, 186
Shopping lists, 65–67
Symptoms, 151

DIGITAL LITERACY, 10, 23, 28, 45, 51, 74, 100, 128, 129, 153, 180, 182

LEARNER LOGS, 29–31, 55–57, 81–83, 138–140, 161–163, 187–189

LIFE SKILLS
Academic goals, 201–203
Advertisements, 49–51
Ailments, 149–151
Asking for assistance, 52–54
Budgets, 104–106
Classified ads, 95–97
Community, 114–116
Descriptions, 46–48
Directions, 126–128
Directory index, 124–125
Doctor's appointments, 152–154
Emergencies, 158–160
Evaluations, 172–174
Family relationships, 17–19
Feelings, 5

Following instructions, 9–11, 78–80, 184–186
Greetings, 3–5
Healthy diet, 75–77
Healthy practices, 146–148
Housing, 92–94
Identify goals, 198–200
Job applications, 178–180
Job descriptions, 175–177
Job interviews, 181–183
Meal planning, 71
Medical labels, 155–157
Menus, 66–68
Messages and letters, 129–133
Personal information, 14–16
Phone numbers, 7, 125
Recipes, 78–80
Registration forms, 6–8
Rental application forms, 98–100
Rooms and furniture, 101–103
Schedules, 23–25
Shopping, 43–45, 49–54
Shopping lists, 69–71
Solving problems, 207–209
Supermarkets, 72–74
Weather, 26–28
Work goals, 204–206
Writing letters and emails, 131–132
Writing down goals, 210–212

TEAM PROJECTS, 35, 61, 87, 113, 141, 167, 193, 219

TOPICS
Classroom, 3–11
Greetings, 3–5
Instructions, 9–11
Registration forms, 6–8
Community, 118–141
Describing community, 118–122
Directions, 126–127
Directory index, 124–125
Messages and letters, 129–133
Writing letters and emails, 131–132
Everyday life, 14–37
Describe people, 20–22
Family relationships, 17–19
Personal information, 14–16
Schedules, 23–25
Weather, 26–28

Explore the Workforce, 29–31, 55–57, 81–83, 107–109, 135–137, 161–163, 187–189, 213–215

Food and nutrition, 66–89
- Healthy foods, 75–77
- Menus, 66–68
- Recipes, 78–80
- Shopping lists, 69–71
- Supermarkets, 72–74

Goals and learning, 198–221
- Academic goals, 201–203
- Identify goals, 198–200
- Record goals, 198–200
- Solve problems, 207–209
- Work goals, 204–206

Health, 144–169
- Ailments, 149–151
- Doctor's appointments, 152–154
- Emergencies, 158–160
- Healthy practices, 146–148
- Medicine labels, 155–157

Housing, 92–115
- Budgets, 104–106
- Classified ads, 95–97
- Rental applications, 98–100
- Rooms and furniture, 101–103
- Types of housing, 92–94

Shopping, 40–63
- Advertisements, 49–51
- Asking for assistance, 52–54
- Asking prices, 43–45
- Describing clothing, 46–48
- Identifying clothes, 40–42

Work, 172–195
- Evaluations, 172–174
- Following instructions, 184–186
- Job applications, 178–180
- Job descriptions, 175–177
- Job interviews, 181–183

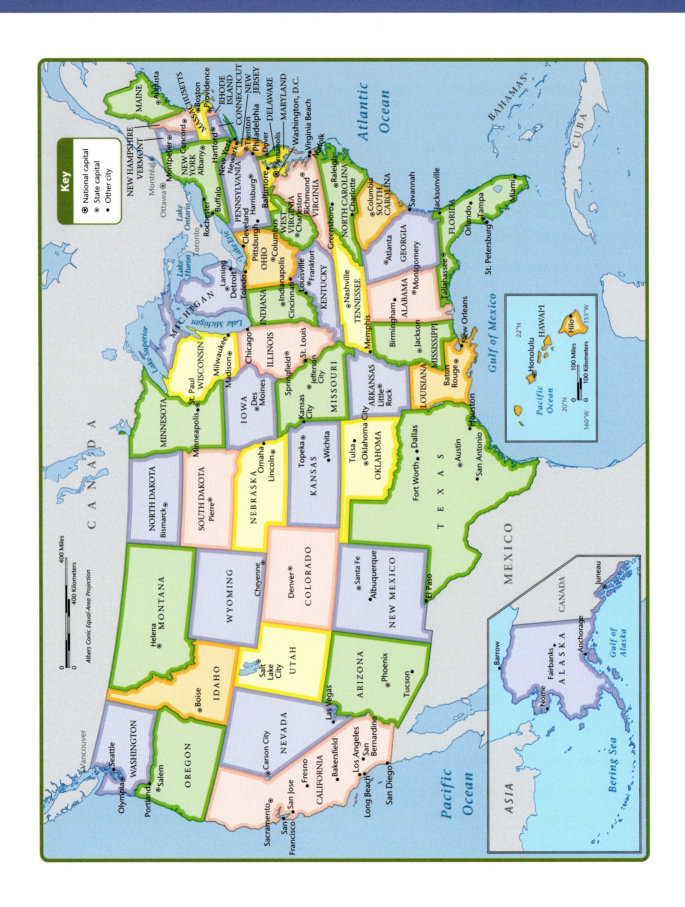

MAP OF THE UNITED STATES